ALP

HABOOK

typeface design & application

general editor • roger walton

ALPHABOOK

First published in 1999 by:
Hearst Books International
1350 Avenue of the Americas
New York, NY 10019
United States of America

Distributed in the United States
and Canada by:
Watson-Guptill Publications
1515 Broadway
New York, NY 10036
Telephone: (800) 451-1741;
(732) 363-4511 in NJ, AK, HI
Fax: (732) 363-0338

Distributed throughout the rest
of the world by:
Hearst Books International
1350 Avenue of the Americas
New York, NY 10019
Fax: (212) 261-6795

ISBN 0-688-16851-5

First published in Germany by:
NIPPAN
Nippon Shuppan Hanbai
Deutschland GmbH
Krefelder Str. 85
D-40549 Düsseldorf
Telephone: (0211) 5048089
Fax: (0211) 5049326

ISBN 3-931884-44-9

Edited and designed by:
Duncan Baird Publishers
75–76 Wells Street, London W1P 3RE

Managing Designer: Gabriella Le Grazie
Designer: Dan Sturges
Editor: Ingrid Court-Jones
Editorial Assistant: James Hodgson
Project Co-ordinator: Tara Solesbury

10 9 8 7 6 5 4 3 2 1

Typeset in Rotis Sans Serif
Color reproduction by Colourscan, Singapore
Printed in Hong Kong

NOTE
All measurements listed in this book
are for width followed by height.

foreword

From the first Western letterforms used by the ancient
Greeks in the fifth century BC to the huge diversity of
typefaces available today, typography has fascinated an
evergrowing, dedicated group of people with an overwhelming
desire to communicate. Now, after centuries of comparatively
slow development, the technological advances of the
computer age enable designers to experiment with new
typefaces with much greater flexibility and speed.

Alphabook is a celebration of all that is best in current
typeface design. Concentrating on the more adventurous
areas of typography, but including bold new text faces as
well as more experimental display pieces, this selection shows
a wide range of work by designers from around the globe.

Innovative, irreverent, and sometimes deliberately

demanding to decipher, the typography featured in *Alphabook*

illustrates a rich variety of typeface designs. Combined with

useful contact details of where to obtain the typefaces

themselves, this is an inspirational and indispensable

collection for designers everywhere.

RW

"The development of new typefaces is a barometer of the stupidity of our profession." Paul Rand

(Please tick appropriate box)

☐ Designer disagrees

☐ Designer agrees

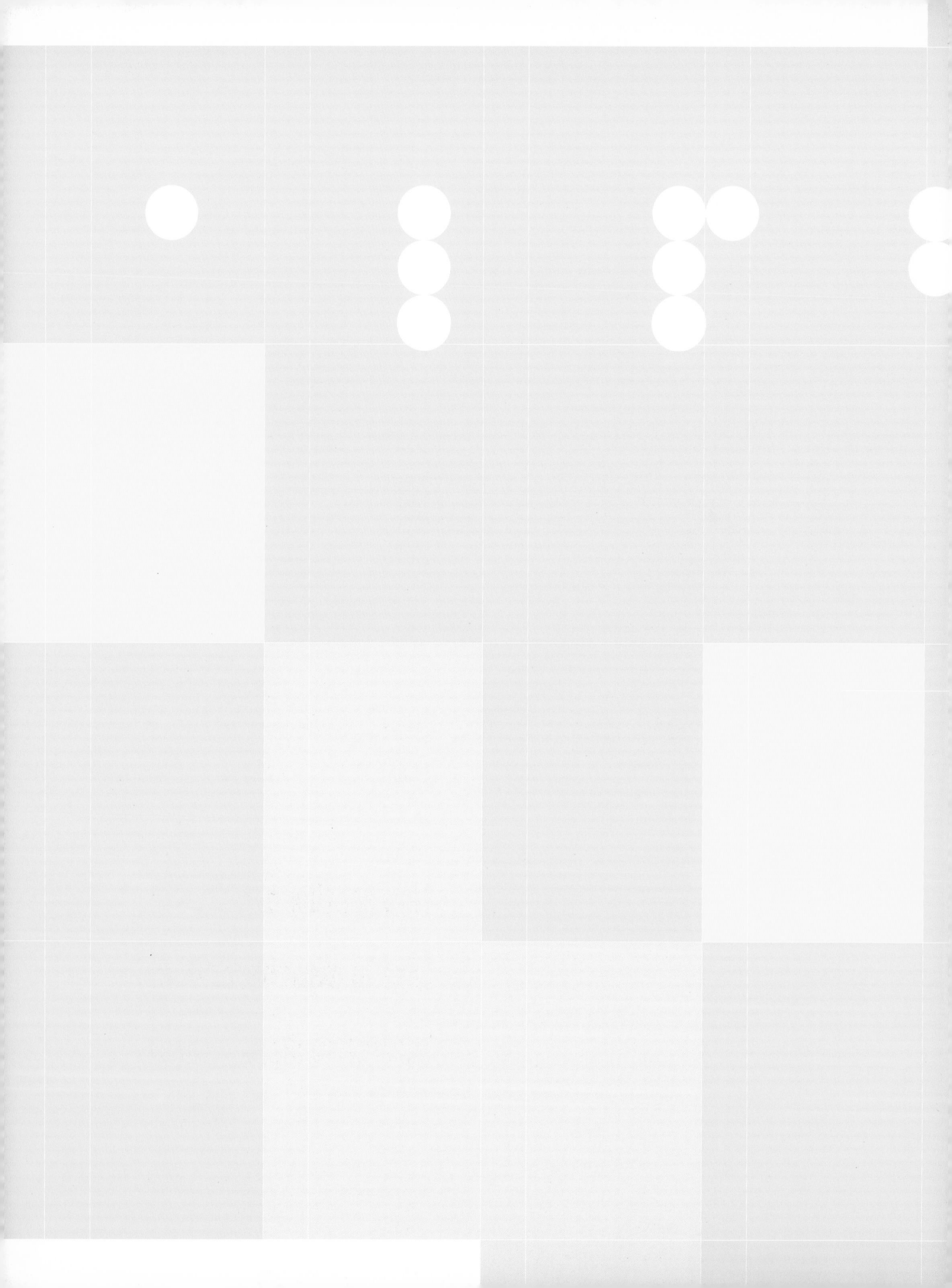

alpha 1

display faces

This section explores the best in experimental and innovative display faces.

typeface
Whiplash
Lineola

typeface family
Whiplash

designer
Bob Aufuldish

foundry/supplier
fontBoy

country of origin
USA

artwork title
Proofs of Catastrophe

typeface
Whiplash

designer
Bob Aufuldish

design company
Aufuldish & Warinner

photographer
Bob Aufuldish

country of origin
USA

description
A book cover for *Proofs of Catastrophe*, a volume of prose poems by Mark Bartlett.

dimensions
127 x 178 mm
5 x 7 in

ABCDE
FGHIJKL
MNOPQRS
TUVWXYZ

abcde
fghijklmn
opqrstu
vwxyz

1234567890 ! @ & * ( ) " ?

doubles
twists
MEANING

the graphic designates the
ectory
along which meaning moves
curves
twists
doubles back or orbits
plying its course under the tw
fluences
of both verbal and visual for

graphic

abcdefghijklmnopqrstuvwxyz

1234567890!@&*()"?

ABCDEFGHISK
LMNOPQRS
TUVWXYZ

typeface
Viscosity Regular

typeface family
Viscosity

designers
Kathy Warinner
and Bob Aufuldish

foundry/supplier
fontBoy

country of origin
USA

artwork title
fontBoy screensaver

typefaces
all fontBoy fonts

designer
Bob Aufuldish

design company
Aufuldish & Warinner

writer
Mark Bartlett

programming
David Karam and
Dave Granvold

country of origin
USA

description
The fontBoy screensaver uses quotes
from Mark Bartlett's essay, "Beyond
the Margins of the Page," juxtaposed
with a soundtrack of snoring. It
connects nine quotations randomly
with seven typefaces (two of which
are illegible), and then selects a
combination to show on-screen.
The quotations, which comment on
the cultural significance of graphic
design, offer a marked contrast to
the mundane activity of work.
(See also pages 100–101)

dimensions
640 x 480 pixels

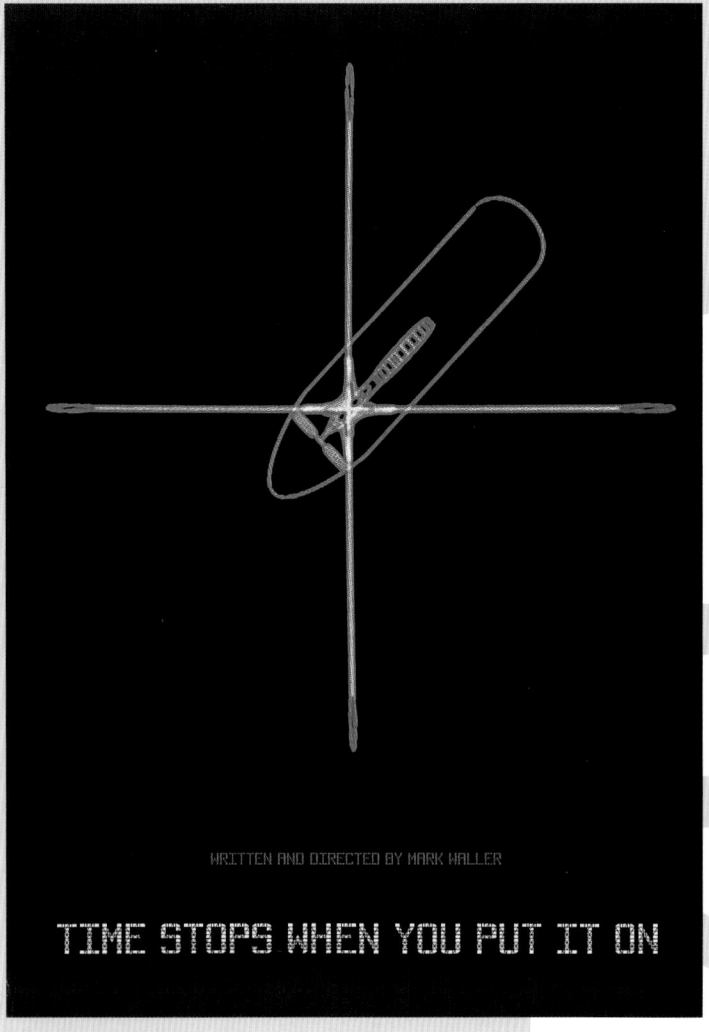

WRITTEN AND DIRECTED BY MARK WALLER

TIME STOPS WHEN YOU PUT IT ON

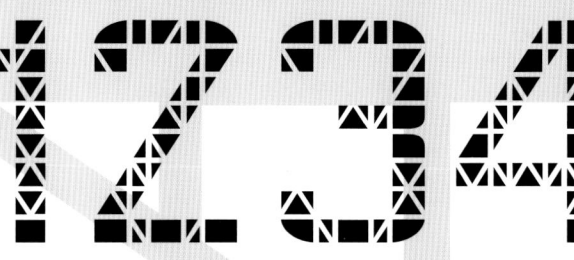

artwork title
Time Stops When
You Put It On

typeface
AF Track Two

designer
Christian Küsters

design company
CHK Design Ltd.

illustrator
Mark Waller

country of origin
UK

description
A poster for the film *Time Stops
When You Put It On*, directed
by Mark Waller.

dimensions
420 x 595 mm
16¹/₂ x 23³/₈ in

ABCDE

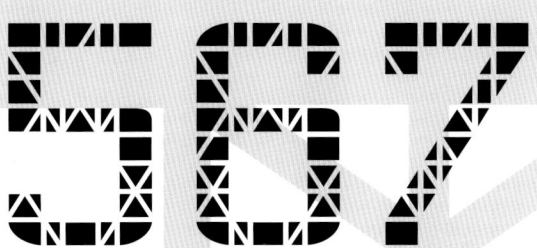

typeface
AF Track Two

typeface family
AF Track Two

designer
Christian Küsters

foundry/supplier
ACME Fonts

country of origin
UK

abcdefghijklmnopqrstuvwxyz

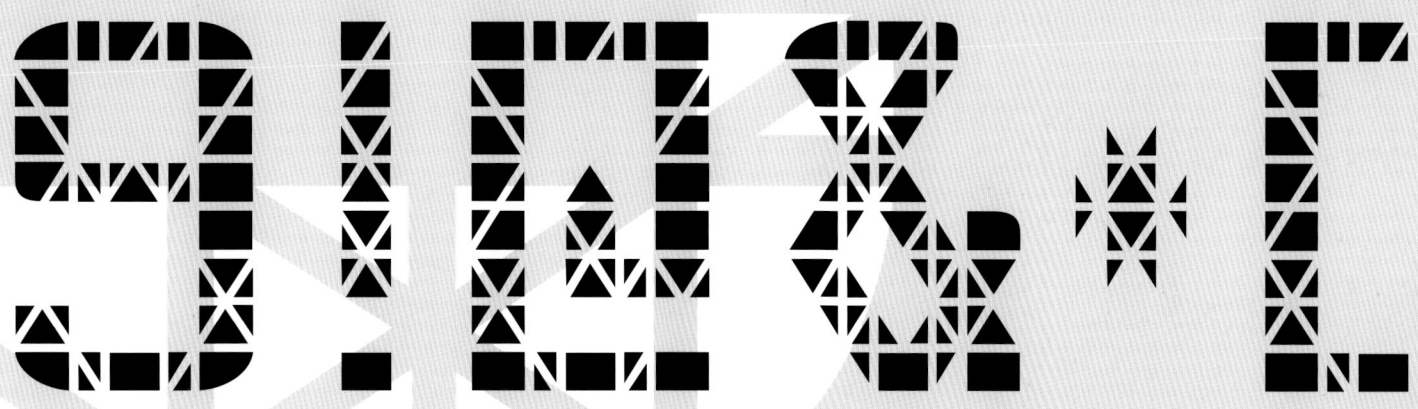

FGHIJKLMNOPQRSTUVWXYZ

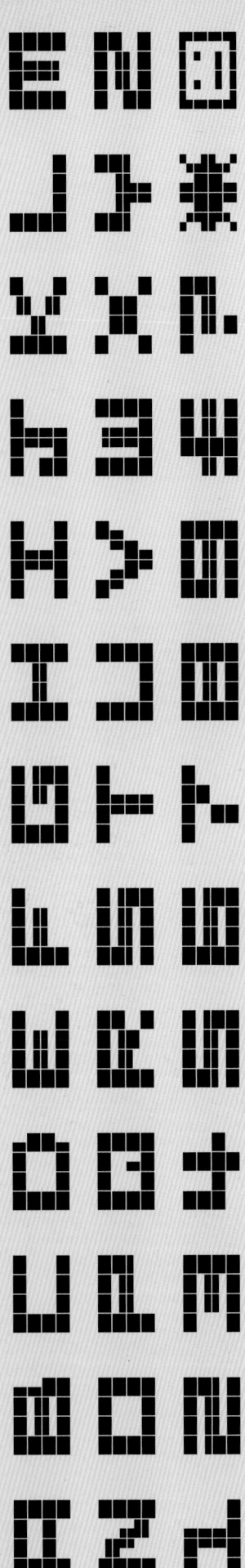

typeface

AF Video Wall

typeface family
AF Video Wall

designer
Anthony Burrill

foundry/supplier
ACME Fonts

country of origin
UK

artwork title
Architectural Association
School of Architecture

typeface
AF Video Wall

designer
Christian Küsters

design company
CHK Design Ltd.

photographer
Paul Wesley Griggs

country of origin
UK

description
A poster promoting the Architectural
Association School of Architecture.

dimensions
420 x 594 mm
16$^1/_2$ x 23$^3/_8$ in

AA

ARCHITECTURA LASSOCIATION

SCHOOL OF ARCHITECTURE

THE AA IS A RADICAL SCHOOL OF ARCHITECTURE WITH A STRONG COMMITMENT TO ADDRESSING THE VITAL ISSUES OF OUR DAY. THE DIVERSITY OF ITS STUDENTS AND STAFF IS REFLECTED IN ITS TEACHING PHILOSOPHY, WHICH ENGAGES WITH THE COMPLEX THEORETICAL, TECHNICAL, ECONOMIC AND POLITICAL ISSUES THAT MAKE UP THE CONTEMPORARY DISCOURSES OF ARCHITECTURE AND URBANISM.

Courses include a five-year programme in architecture leading to RIBA Parts 1 and 2 and the AA Diploma; a one-year Open Unit/Foundation course; the Graduate Design programme (in Architecture and Urbanism / Landscape Urbanism); full-time postgraduate courses in Environment and Energy, Histories and Theories of Architecture, Housing and Urbanism; and professional courses in Building Conservation, Conservation of Historic Gardens and Landscapes, Environmental Access, and Professional Practice (RIBA Part 3).

For further information (including details of scholarships) please contact:
The Admissions Office
AA School of Architecture
36 Bedford Square
London WC1B 3ES
T (+44) 171 887 4000
F (+44) 171 414 0782
arch-assoc@arch-assoc.co.uk

Design CHK Design Ltd Photography Paul Wesley Griggs

typeface

Velvet Velour

typeface family
Velvet

designer
Charles Wilkin

foundry/supplier
Prototype Experimental Foundry

country of origin
USA

123456789O Laa&*GD"?

artwork title
Delicious Again

typeface
Velvet Velour

designer
Charles Wilkin

design company
Automatic Art and Design

country of origin
USA

description
A direct mail poster featuring
the typeface Velvet Velour.

dimensions
273 x 425 mm
10³/₄ x 16³/₄ in

AB CD

typeface

Superchunk

typeface family
Superchunk

designer
Charles Wilkin

foundry/supplier
Prototype Experimental Foundry

country of origin
USA

EFGHI JKLMNO PQRST UVWXYZ

1234567890!@&()"?

artwork title	design company	description	dimensions
1996 CSCA Creative Best Catalog	Automatic Art and Design	A spread from the Columbus Society of Communicating Arts Creative Best Catalog, which showcases the winners of the Columbus Society annual competition. By reassembling the winning entries into a collage, which were then used as graphics throughout the book, the 1996 catalog became a representation of the exhibition while still retaining its own identity.	291 x 184 mm 11¹/₂ x 7¹/₄ in
typeface Superchunk	**illustrator** Charles Wilkin		
designer Charles Wilkin	**country of origin** USA		

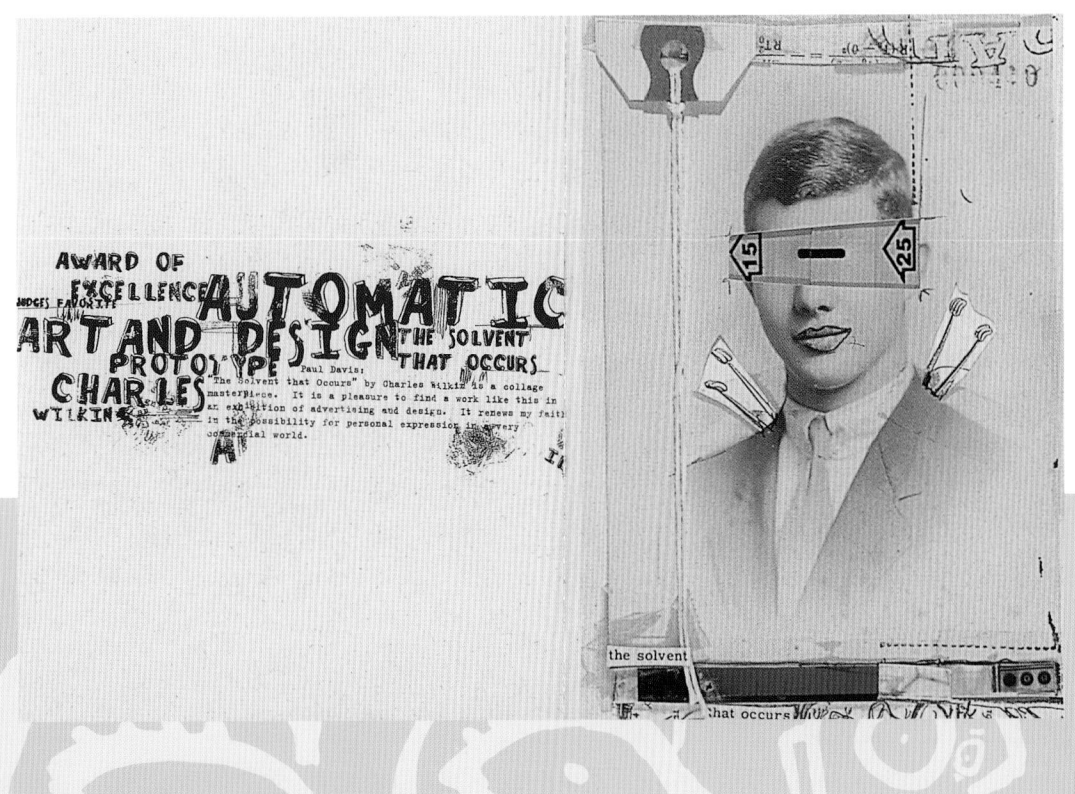

abcdefghijklmn
opqrstuvwxyz
1234567890
!&*()"?

typeface

Smack

typeface family
Smack

designer
Jill Bell

foundry/supplier
International Typeface Corporation

country of origin
USA

artwork title
Counting Crows

typeface
Smack

art directors
Bill Merryfield and Robin Sloan

designer
Bill Merryfield

design company
Geffen Records

photographers
Sarah Moon and Chris Strother

country of origin
USA

description
CD and CD cover

dimensions
CD: 120 mm, 4³/₄ in diameter
CD cover: 120 x 120 mm,
4³/₄ x 4³/₄ in

A B C D E F G H
I J K L M N O P Q
R S T U V W X Y Z

abcde
fghijklm
nopqrstu
vwxyz

typeface
Gigi

typeface family
Gigi

designer
Jill Bell

foundry/supplier
International Typeface Corporation

country of origin
USA

artwork title
Sylvia's Romantic Reminder

typeface
Gigi

designer
Tom Greensfelder

design company
Tom Greensfelder

illustrator
Nicole Hollander

country of origin
USA

description
Illustrations for a 1998 calendar

dimensions
305 x 305 mm
12 x 12 in

1234567890!&*()"?

ABCDEFGHIJKLMNOPQRSTUVWXYZ

artwork title
Lo-fi Coffee

typeface
Bigson 0.01

designer
James Gibson

design company
j-buyers.com

photographer
James Gibson

illustrator
James Gibson

country of origin
UK

description
One of three pages in a design
collaboration between j-buyers.com
and suction.com, shown on the
internet in autumn 1998.

dimensions
600 x 350 pixels

34567890 @

ABCDE
FGHIJKL
NOPQR
STUVV
WXYZ

typeface

Bigson 0.01

typeface family
Bigson

designer
James Gibson

foundry/supplier
j-buyers.com

country of origin
UK

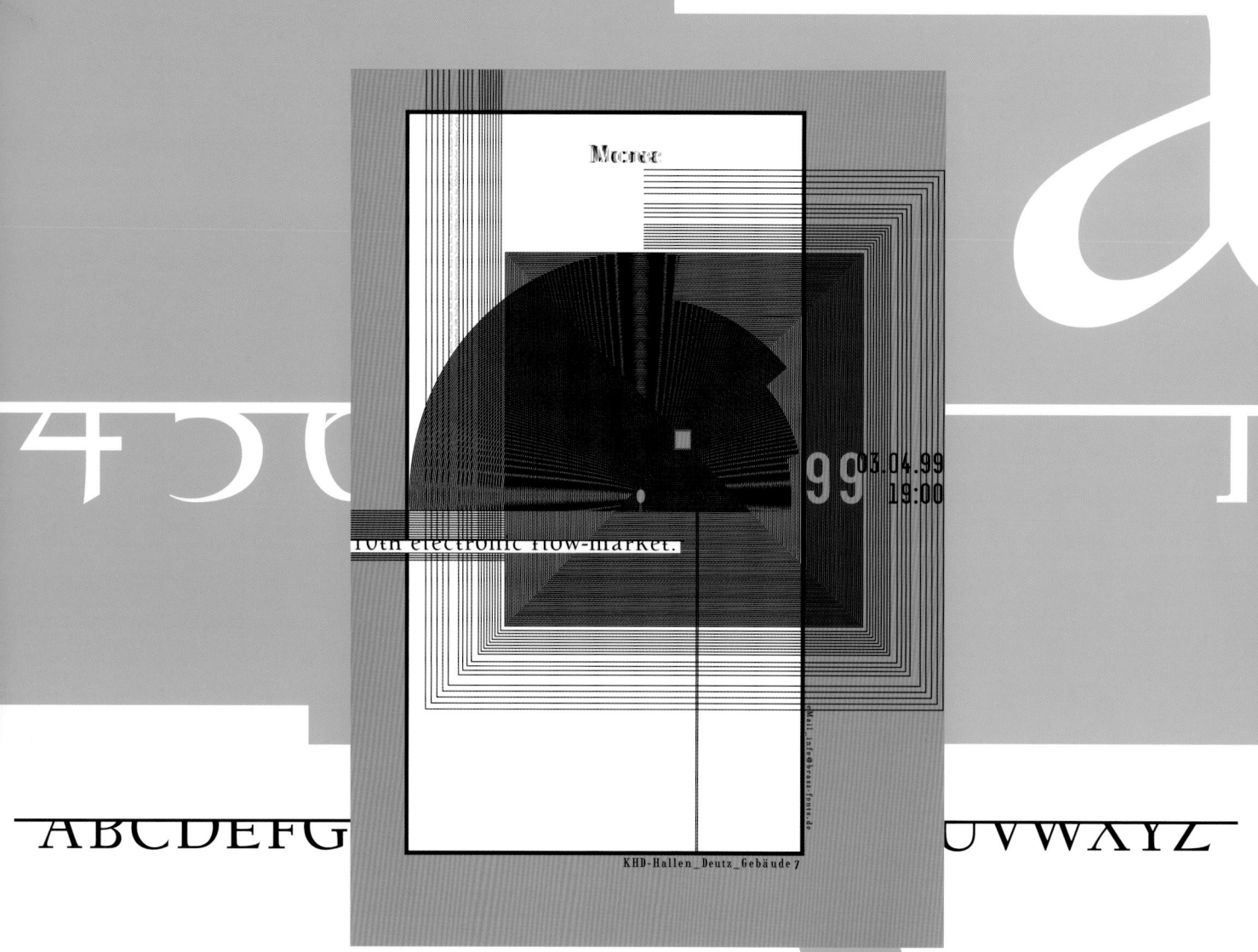

artwork title
Electronic Flow-Market

typeface
bf_SubZero

designer
Andrea Markewitz

design company
godz advertising_cologne

illustrator
Andrea Markewitz

country of origin
Germany

description
A poster for the "Moirée," a music fair which specializes in used LPs and CDs, and offers the opportunity to mix new styles of electronic music on turntables.

dimensions
594 x 840 mm
$23^3/_8$ x $33^1/_8$ in

1234567890!@&*()"?

ABCDEFGHIJKLMNOPQRSTUVWXYZ

d

rstuvwxyz

1234567890

!@&*()"?

typeface
bf_SubZero

typeface family
bf_SubZero

designer
Guido Schneider

foundry/supplier
brass_fonts cologne

country of origin
Germany

29

1234567890!(]'"?

abcdef

ghijklmnopqr

stuvwxyz

typeface

BD Fazer

typeface family
BD Fazer

designer
MBrunner

foundry/supplier
Apply Design Group

country of origin
Switzerland

artwork title
TypeFace#4

typeface
BD Fazer

art director
MBrunner

designer
Lopetz

design company
büro destruct

country of origin
Switzerland

description
An image from the büro destruct
TypeFace exhibition.

dimensions
1000 x 1000 mm
39³/₈ x 39³/₈ in

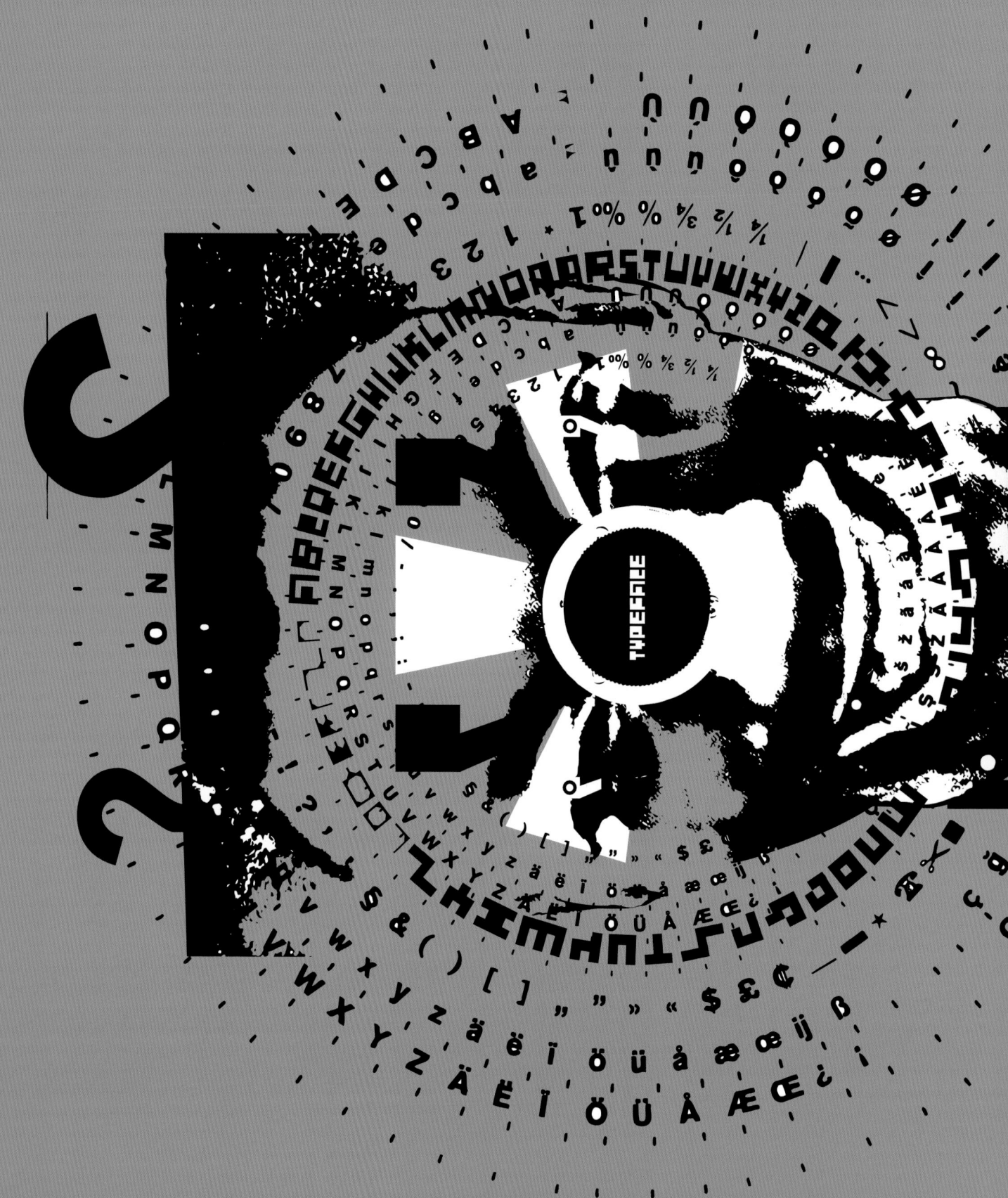

artwork title
TypeFace#3

typeface
BD Lodel Fizler

art director
Lopetz

designer
MBrunner

design company
büro destruct

country of origin
Switzerland

description
as on previous spread

dimensions
1000 x 1000 mm
$39^3/_8$ x $39^3/_8$ in

typeface
BD Lodel Fizler

typeface family
BD Lodel Fizler

designer
Lopetz

foundry/supplier
büro destruct

country of origin
Switzerland

1234567 0

artwork title
TypeFace#5

typeface
BD Doomed SquareUp

designer
MBrunner

design company
büro destruct

country of origin
Switzerland

description
as on page 31

dimensions
1000 x 1000 mm
$39^3/_8$ x $39^3/_8$ in

abcdefghijklmnopqrstuvwxyz

artwork title
Strategic Planning

typeface
Crate

designer
Gerry Chapleski

design company
Gerry Chapleski Design

country of origin
USA

description
Typographic visual play is used to catch the eye on this brochure cover promoting a company's plans for attracting new business.

dimensions
216 x 216 mm
8¹/₂ x 8¹/₂ in

2   August 1997

STRATEGIC
PLANNING

PROCESS

typeface

Ballerina

typeface family
Ballerina

designer
Sean Fermoyle

foundry/supplier
Sean Fermoyle

country of origin
USA

artwork title
Ballerina

typeface
Ballerina

designer
Sean Fermoyle

design company
Sean Fermoyle

photographer
Sean Fermoyle

country of origin
USA

description
A promotional image to display a well-balanced typeface with elegant flair and counter-weight.

dimensions
406 x 203 mm
16 x 8 in

typeface

Disco

typeface family
Disco

designer
Sean Fermoyle

foundry/supplier
Attention Earthling

country of origin
USA

artwork title
It's All About the Disco

typeface
Disco

designer
Sean Fermoyle

design company
Sean Fermoyle

photographers
Sean Fermoyle and
Yumi Minamikurosawa

country of origin
USA

description
A promotional image featuring the
Disco typeface, which seeks to echo
the meshing of circular beats and
rhythms. It was influenced by
the designer's experience as a DJ.

dimensions
203 x 203 mm
8 x 8 in

abcdefghij

Klmnö

artwork title
Atmosphere

typeface
Atmosphere

designer
Sean Fermoyle

design company
Sean Fermoyle

photographer
Sean Fermoyle

country of origin
USA

description
The forms represented by "Atmosphere" capture the feel of a futuristic and hieroglyphic typeface of the kind that may be found one day on an American UFO.

dimensions
203 x 203 mm
8 x 8 in

12 3 4

abcdefghijklmnopqrstuvwxyz

ABCDEF
GHIJKLMN
OPQRST
UVWXYZ

1234567890!@&* { } " ?

typeface

Atmosphere

typeface family
Atmosphere

designers
Sean Fermoyle and Jason Carberry

foundry/supplier
Sean Fermoyle

country of origin
USA

abcdefghij

typeface

Milky

typeface family
Milky

designers
Sean Fermoyle and Phoebe Fisher

foundry/supplier
Sean Fermoyle

country of origin
USA

1234567890!?

klm

Nopqrstuv wxyz

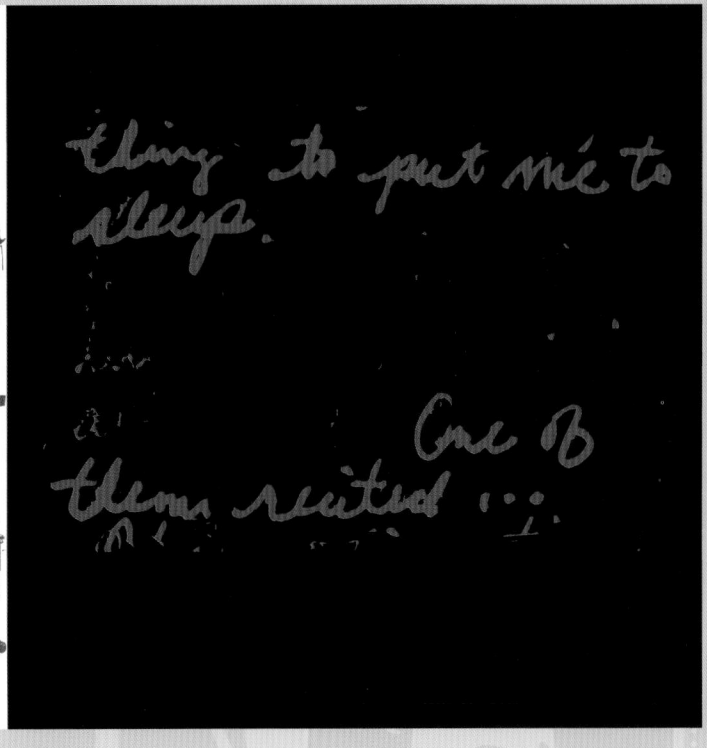

artwork title
Promotional image

typeface
Milky

designer
Sean Fermoyle

design company
Sean Fermoyle

illustrator
Phoebe Fisher

country of origin
USA

description
Phoebe Fisher's illustrations for clubs and parties were digitized in this promotional image to capture the feel of a hand-drawn urban flyer.

dimensions
406 x 203 mm
16 x 8 in

abcdefghijklmnopqrstuvwxyz
1234567890!?@#*

typeface
Neuphoric
Regular

typeface family
Neuphoric

designers
Lee Basford and James Glover
at Fluid UK

foundry/supplier
Fountain

country of origin
UK

abcdefghijklm
nopqrstuvwxyz

artwork title
IMG SRC 100/Fountain

typeface
Neuphoric

designer
Peter Bruhn

design company
Fountain

photographer
Peter Bruhn

country of origin
Sweden

description
An image created for *IMG SRC 100*,
a Japanese design book.

dimensions
405 x 524 mm
16 x 20⅝ in

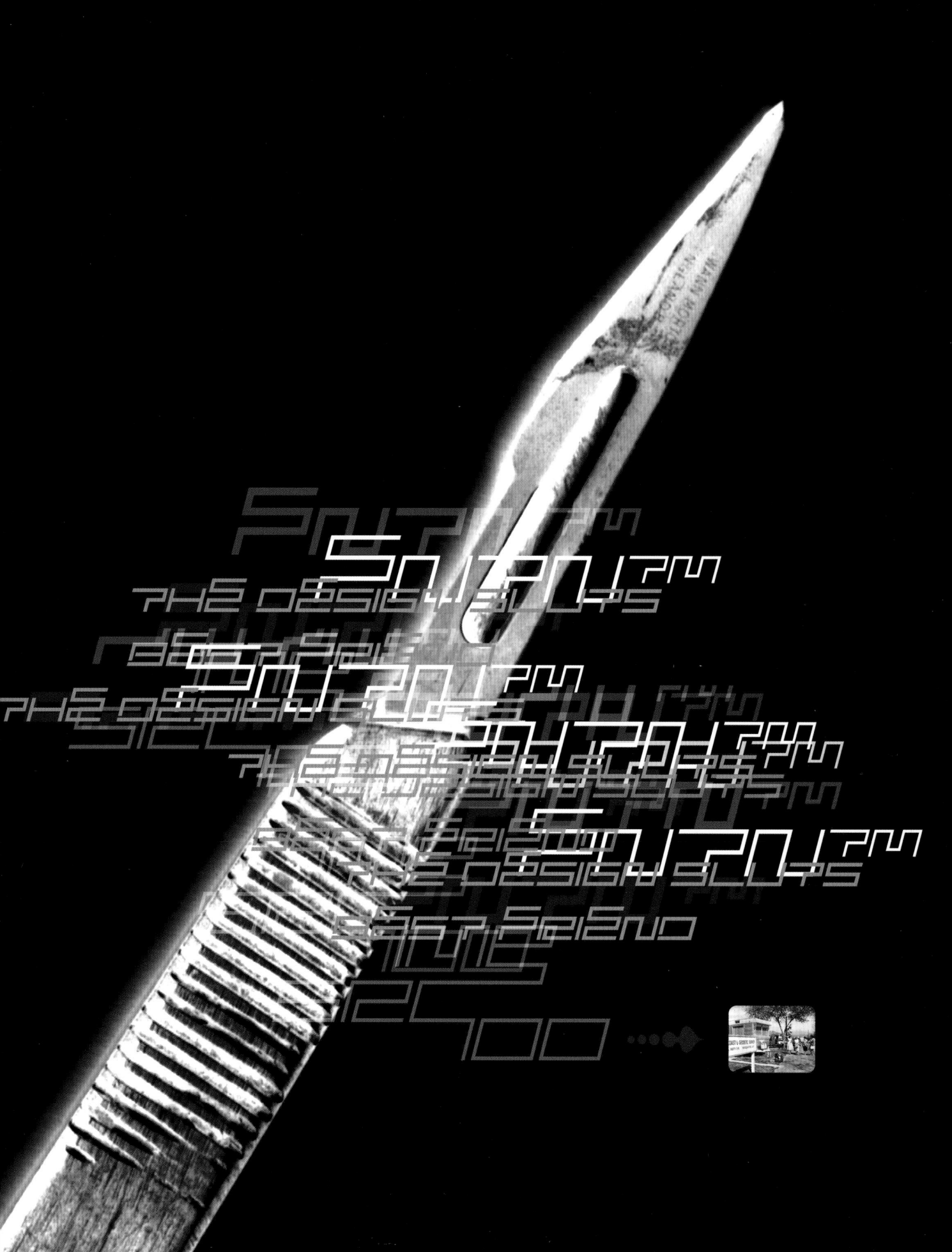

A B C D
I J K L
Q R S
W X

E F G H
M N O P
T U V
Y Z

EBERHARD BLUM VISUAL WORK 1980-98

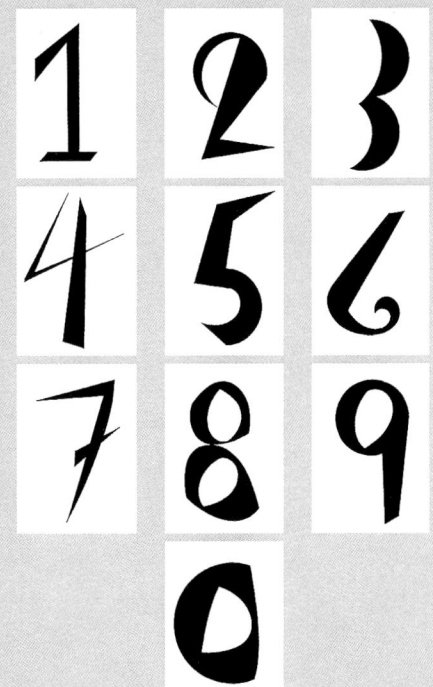

Here, and previous spread:

typeface

Blum

typeface family
Blum

designer
Eberhard Blum

foundry/supplier
not available for commercial use

country of origin
Germany

artwork title
Eberhard Blum Visual Work
1980–1998

typeface
Blum

designer
Ann Holyoke Lehmann

design company
Ann Holyoke Lehmann

country of origin
Germany

description
Cover for an Eberhard Blum catalog

dimensions
210 x 280 mm
8¹/₄ x 11 in

You hear the screaming and sirens out of the half-opened window.
T.V.'s switched on. You're alone. Bored.
Pissed off.

[10:33 pm]

[9:12 pm]

You decide
to **shoot**. You feel the

Now the noise outside sounds sweeter in
your ears. You're sitting comfortably.
You're in your world now.
Your rules.
No fear.

Especially the pain.
It kills the pain for a few hours.

[8:03 pm]
cold used needle piercing your skin.   They call you a junkhead.
You don't care. Soon it'll be heaven.   They laugh
at you.
What do they know? They've never been
where you've been.

No pain.

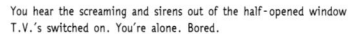

[11:08 pm]

Everything seems so worthless now.
You smile. You feel strong. Nobody
can hurt you...

[12:12 pm]

It's now past midnight.
Music's off.
There's a depressing silence. You sit on the couch unable to move.

Wishing your life was over.
One day you might pull the trigger...

Staring.

Yeah, well.
It's all fun and games
'til somebody gets **hurt.**

[*CHOOSE LIFE* ]

artwork title
Choose Life

country of origin
UK

typefaces
Streetwise Scarred and
Praktic Gothic

designer
Michael Loizides

design company
NOISE

photographer
Michael Loizides

description
Imagery is reduced to a minimum
and type is used as the main vehicle
of expression to convey the anti-
drugs message in this poster.

dimensions
1188 x 840 mm
46³/₄ x 33¹/₈ in

abcdefghijklmnopqrstuvwxyz

1234567890!@&*( )"?

ABCDEFGHIJKLMNOPQRSTUVWXYZ

typeface
Streetwise Scarred

typeface family
Streetwise Scarred

designer
Michael Loizides

foundry/supplier
NOISE

country of origin
UK

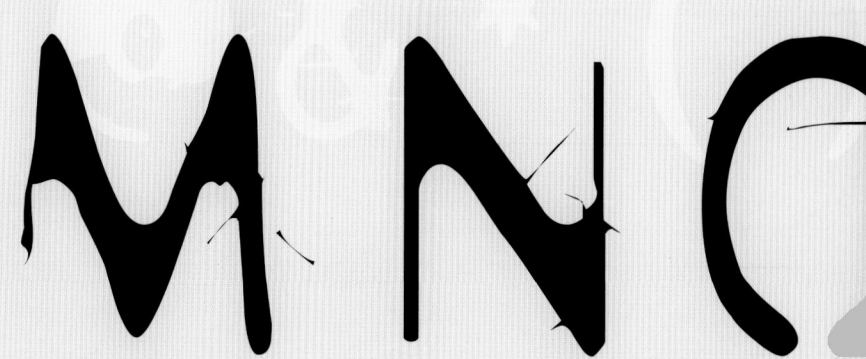

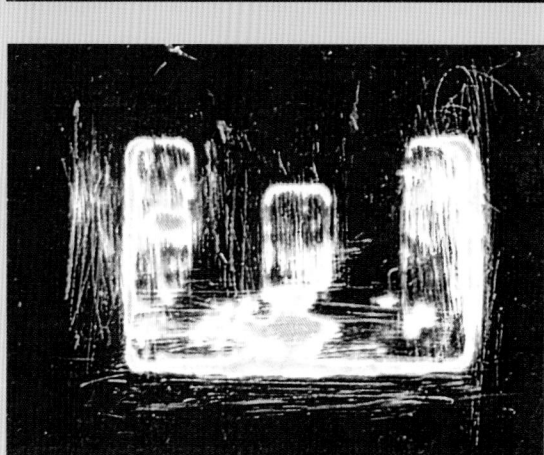

description

This work was created by
sandpapering photographic paper
to reveal the hidden layers of
pigment underneath. It fuses
type with image to combine
two channels of communication:
seeing and reading, so that the
viewer experiences the piece in
two different ways simultaneously.
The designer refers to his work as
"photo-typography."

dimensions

not applicable

artwork title
Fire

typeface
Fire

designer
Craig Yamey

design company
YAM

photographer
Craig Yamey

country of origin
UK

typeface

Fire

typeface family
Fire

designer
Craig Yamey

foundry/supplier
YAM

country of origin
UK

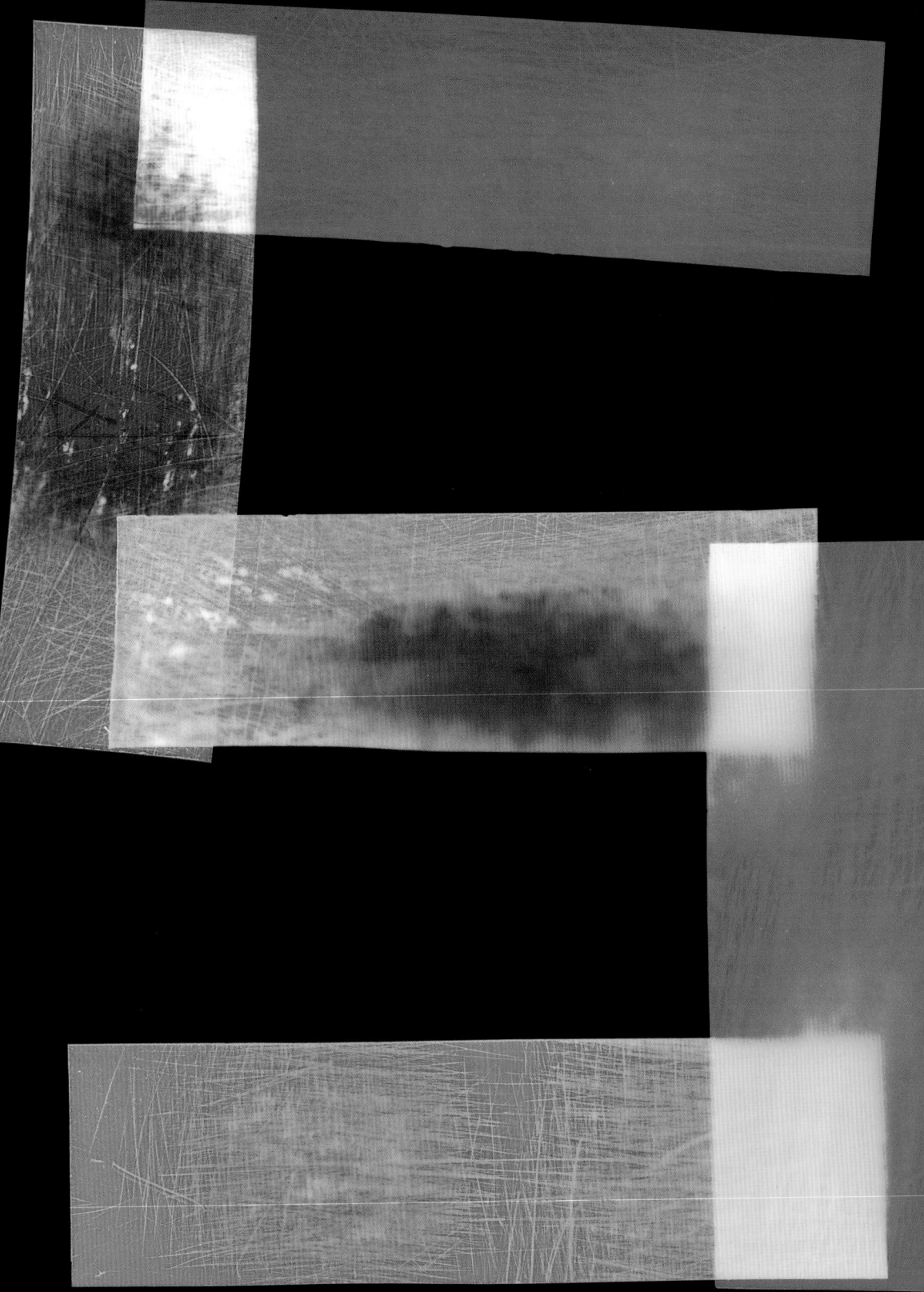

 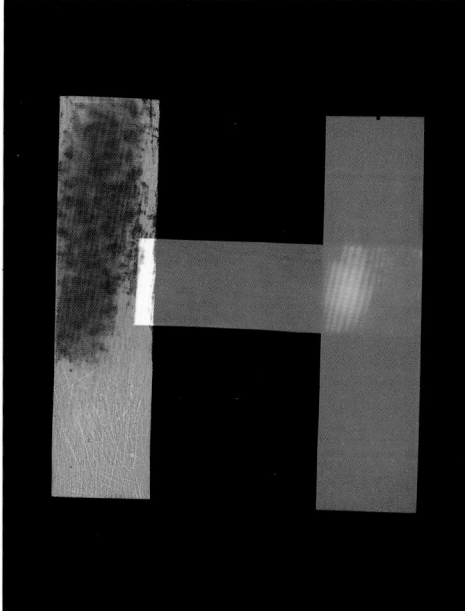 

typeface

Striplight

typeface family
Striplight

designer
Craig Yamey

foundry/supplier
YAM

country of origin
UK

artwork title
Striplight

typeface
Striplight

designer
Craig Yamey

design company
YAM

photographer
Craig Yamey

country of origin
UK

description
Constructed with photograms of acetate strips, a varying intensity of color is created in this work through using different light exposures. Because the acetate is laid onto photographic paper in total darkness, the alphabet is made by feeling the shape of the letters.

dimensions
not applicable

artwork title
Scratch

typeface
Scratch

designer
Craig Yamey

design company
YAM

photographer
Craig Yamey

country of origin
UK

description
This alphabet was produced by
scratching negatives with different
grades of sandpaper. They were
then put through a photographic
enlarger to develop the particular
characteristics of each letter.

dimensions
not applicable

typeface

Scratch

typeface family
Scratch

designer
Craig Yamey

foundry/supplier
YAM

country of origin
UK

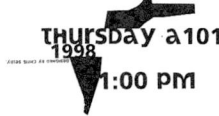

abcdef

123

artwork title
Martin Venezky Visiting Designer

typefaces
Outsider and Flair

designer
Chris Selby

design company
Chris Selby Design

illustrator
Chris Selby

country of origin
USA

description
In this poster advertising a lecture by Martin Venezky, the style of the typefaces reflects Venezky's work. His name has been deliberately misspelt, then pasted over as a reference to his love of errors. The different style of the letter "z" refers to Venezky's commercial art background, while Outsider's wild character suggests Venezky's unorthodox methods.

dimensions
585 x 890 mm
23 x 35 in

ghijklmnopqrstuvwxyz

ABCDEFGHIJKLMNOPQRSTUVWXYZ

456789

typeface

Outsider

typeface family
Outsider

designer
Chris Selby

foundry/supplier
Chris Selby

country of origin
USA

1234567890 !&"?

natural DISaster RIDE in a MUltipurpose-box

(THUNDER AND LIGHTNING IN THE GROCERYSECTION)

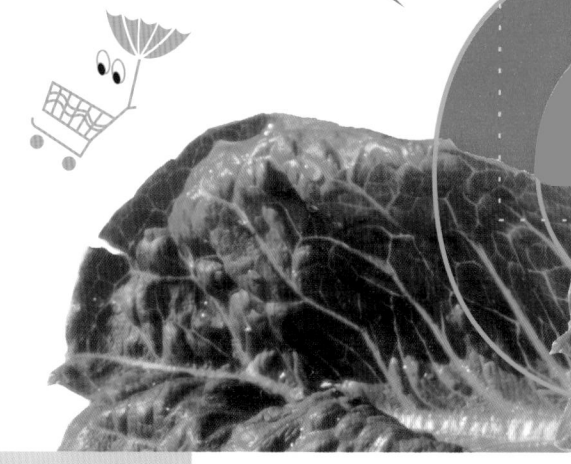

artwork title
Alien Habits or Speculations On
Drive-by Observations

typefaces
rolypoly supreme, Clarendon,
and Rosewood Fill

designer
Pirco Wolfframm

college
California Institute of the Arts

photographer
Pirco Wolfframm

country of origin
Germany/USA

description
A spread from the Small World
section of a final project at graduate
school, exploring how the designer's
attitudes to everyday Californian
life have been influenced by her
German upbringing.

dimensions
381 x 178 mm
15 x 7¹/₈ in

abcdefghijklmnopqrstuvwxyz

ABCDEF
GHIJKLM
NOPQRST
UVWXYZ

typeface

rolypoly supreme

typeface family
rolypoly supreme

designer
Pirco Wolfframm

foundry/supplier
Pirco Wolfframm

country of origin
Germany/USA

JOSTICS

artwork title
Evolution

typeface
KingDumb

designer
David Harlan

design company
popglory

country of origin
USA

description
This work demonstrates the
development of a typeface
from initial sketches through
to finished design.

dimensions
229 x 330 mm
9 x 13 in

typeface

KingDumb

typeface family
KingDumb

designer
David Harlan

foundry/supplier
popglory

country of origin
USA

abcdef
ghijklm
nopqrst
uvwxyz

typeface
Futures

typeface family
Futures

designer
Stephen Banham

foundry/supplier
The Letterbox

country of origin
Australia

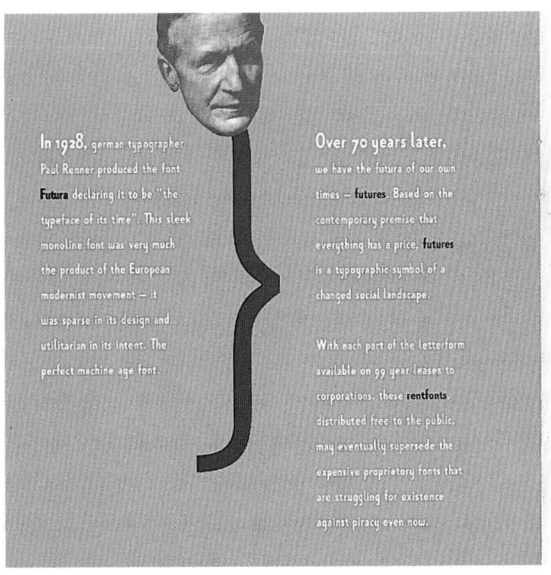

In 1928, german typographer Paul Renner produced the font **Futura** declaring it to be "the typeface of its time". This sleek monoline font was very much the product of the European modernist movement — it was sparse in its design and utilitarian in its intent. The perfect machine age font.

Over 70 years later, we have the futura of our own times — **futures**. Based on the contemporary premise that everything has a price, **futures** is a typographic symbol of a changed social landscape.

With each part of the letterform available on 99 year leases to corporations, these **rentfonts** distributed free to the public, may eventually supersede the expensive proprietary fonts that are struggling for existence against piracy even now.

artwork title
Rentfont

typefaces
Futures and Gaberdine

designer
Stephen Banham

design company
The Letterbox

country of origin
Australia

description
The Rentfont project is based on the notion of reversing the process of creating a corporate identity. As the most effective logos are often seen as images rather than read as type, in assembling the Futures typeface from the parts of a variety of company logos, the idea is to convey the corporate image in the typeface itself.

dimensions
290 x 145 mm
11$\frac{1}{2}$ x 5$\frac{3}{4}$ in

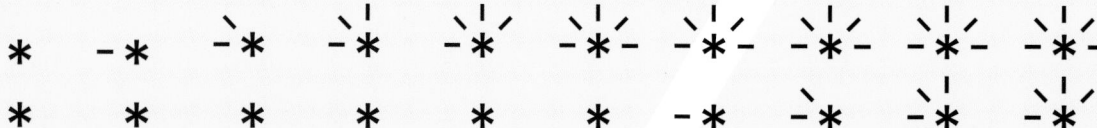

artwork title
FUSE 14 "Cyber" Edition

typefaces
MMMteurs Real and
MMMteurs Cyber

designers
Moniteurs

design company
Moniteurs

country of origin
Germany

description
A poster designed for FUSE 14,
the "Cyber" edition, a "magazine"
published randomly in different
formats. It explores new possibilities
in digital communication and
features the typeface family
MMMteurs, which was invented
as a tribute to information codes
such as ASCII.

dimensions
149 x 210 mm
$5^7/_8 \times 8^1/_4$ in

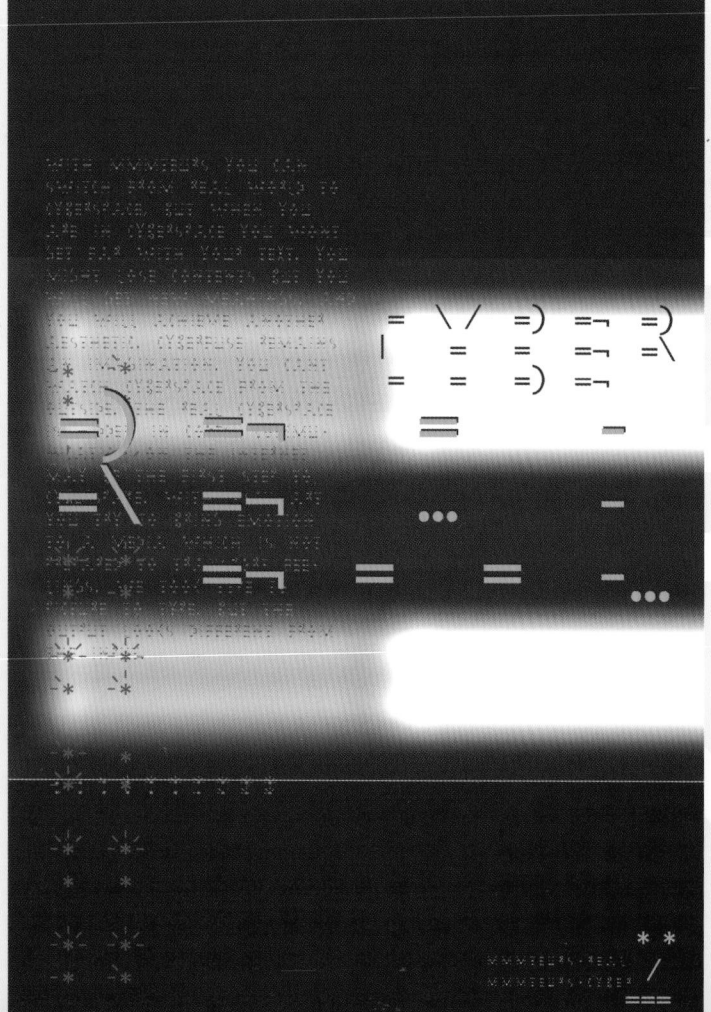

typeface

MMMteurs Real

typeface family
MMMteurs

designers
Heike Nehl, Sibylle Schlaich,
Heidi Specker

foundry/supplier
FontShop International

country of origin
Germany

typeface

F2F Money Mix

typeface family
F2F Money Mix

designers
Moniteurs

foundry/supplier
not available for commercial use

country of origin
Germany

artwork title
F2F "Data Bank" Notes

typeface
F2F Money Mix

designers
Moniteurs

design company
Moniteurs

country of origin
Germany

description
These "data bank" notes were designed for the TYPO '98 conference in Berlin. The special F2F Money Mix typeface—a remix of Face2Face No.5 fonts—was released at the Moniteurs' live performance at the conference.

dimensions
100MMM and 50MMM notes:
134 x 68 mm, 5$\frac{1}{4}$ x 2$\frac{3}{4}$ in
10MMM note:
125 x 54 mm, 4$\frac{7}{8}$ x 2$\frac{1}{8}$ in

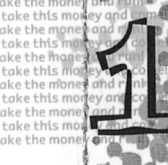

13 03 98 16:30 TYPOstage

take this money and come!

100 MMM

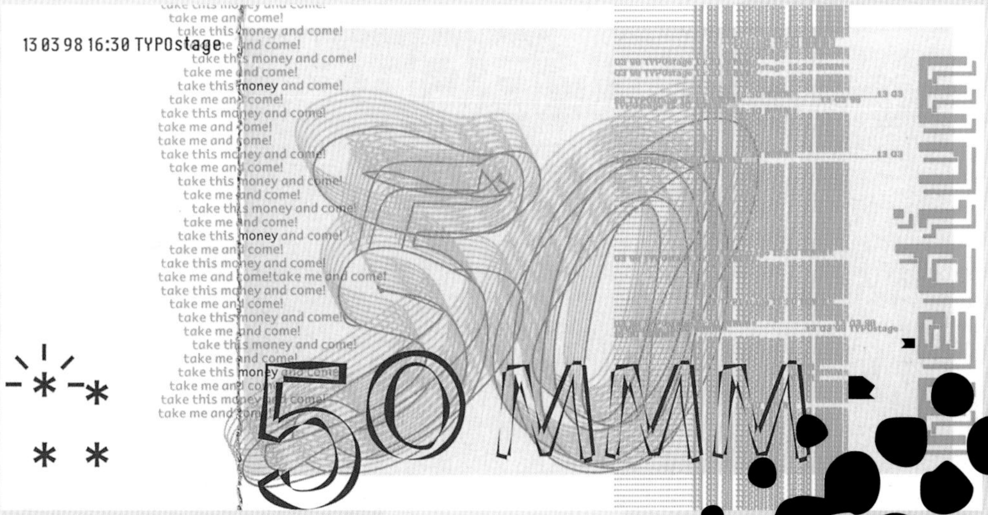

maxi

13 03 98 16:30 TYPOstage

take this money and come!
take me and come!

50 MMM

medium

MMM mini

artwork title
Scarf for *Face2Face* Issue No.3

typefaces
F2F Lego Stoned and F2F Twins

designer
Heike Nehl

design company
Moniteurs

country of origin
Germany

description
This scarf is part of the third issue of
Face2Face, a promotional publication,
which has been published in various
media since the inception of the
Face2Face font foundry in 1993.

dimensions
1690 x 300 mm
66^1/$_2$ x 11^3/$_4$ in

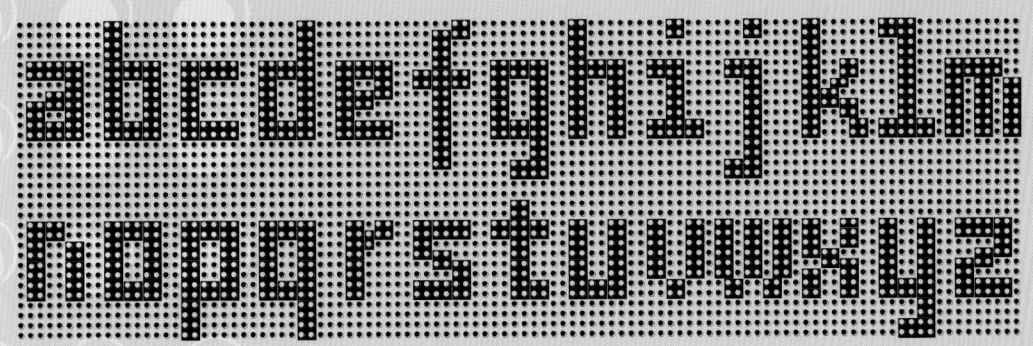

typeface

F2F Lego
Stoned

typeface family
F2F Lego Stoned

designer
Heike Nehl

foundry/supplier
Face2Face

country of origin
Germany

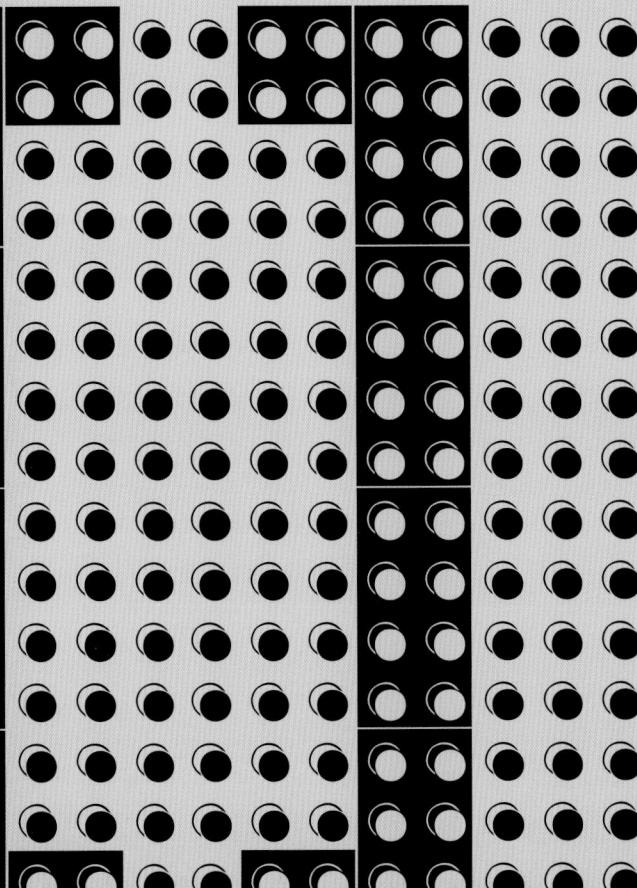

typeface
Antionette

typeface family
Antionette

designer
Lee Schulz

foundry/supplier
Lee Schulz

country of origin
USA

artwork title
Drowning by Ornament

typefaces
Antionette and Salomé

designer
Lee Schulz

design company
Lee Schulz

photographer
Lee Schulz

country of origin
USA

description
Above and right: Rosetta pattern.
Iris prints on watercolor paper
from a thesis entitled "Drowning
by Ornament," featuring typeface
designs based on the ornamentation
of past eras.

dimensions
279 x 419 mm
11 x 16^1/$_2$ in

typeface

Salomé

typeface family
Salomé

designer
Lee Schulz

foundry/supplier
Lee Schulz

country of origin
USA

artwork title
Drowning by Ornament

typefaces
Salomé and Antionette

designer
Lee Schulz

design company
Lee Schulz

photographer
Lee Schulz

country of origin
USA

description
Above left: Skeletal pattern.
Right: Rosetta pattern. Description
as on previous spread.

dimensions
279 x 419 mm
11 x 16$^1/_2$ in

ABCDEFGHIJKLM
NOPQRSTUVWXYZ

artwork title
Architype 3

typeface
Architype Stedelijk

designers
David Quay and Tim Lam Tang

design company
The Foundry

country of origin
UK

description
An advertisement, which appeared in *Eye* magazine, to promote the Architype 3 collection of typefaces.

dimensions
237 x 297 mm
9³/₈ x 11³/₄ in

Architype 3 is the latest collection of avant garde typefaces released by The Foundry, available direct from The Foundry designers Freda Sack & David Quay.

This typeface collection has been developed by The Foundry designers in close collaboration with Wim Crouwel, who originally produced these designs in the late sixties. With his strong interest in grids and techniques Crouwel worked, within the constraints of the electronic technology available, to produce letterforms that worked with, rather than against, the mechanical means that conveyed them.

New Alphabet was his most radical experiment, conceived in response to his experience of the first device for electronic typesetting; characters were specifically designed to follow the underlying dot-matrix system.

Stedelijk appeared on one of Crouwel's seminal posters of the period for the Stedelijk Museum in Amsterdam.

Fodor was designed for a series of catalogue covers for the Fodor Museum, Amsterdam.

Gridnik was originally designed as a typewriter typeface but was never released. A modified version of it can be seen on Crouwel's stamps for the Dutch post office.

Foundry Gridnik is available for both Mac and PC and can be purchased directly from The Foundry designers.

For more information about The Foundry fonts and specially commissioned typefaces, contact designers David Quay and Freda Sack at the following address

The Foundry
Studio 12
10 – 11 Archer Street
London W1V 7HG
England

t 44 (0)171 734 6925
f 44 (0)171 734 2607
e dqfs@thefoundrystudio.co.uk

crouwel collection
architype 3

Architype Gridnik

architype fodor

architype stedelijk

Architype new Alphabet 1

Architype new Alphabet 2

Architype new Alphabet 3

typeface

Architype Stedelijk

typeface family
Architype Stedelijk

designers
Wim Crouwel/The Foundry

foundry/supplier
The Foundry

country of origin
UK

1234567890!+[]'?

abcdefghijklmnopqrstuvwxyz

typeface

Pace Optic One
Black

typeface family
Pace Optic One

designer
Michael Chang Winterberg

foundry/supplier
Pacesetters

country of origin
Denmark

1234567890!@&*()"?

ABCDE
FGHIJKLMNOP
QRSTUVWXYZ

artwork title
Visuals Magazine

typefaces
Pace Optic One, Pace Optic Two,
Pace To Bold, Pace 5, Pace In Love,
and Pace Funky Beep

designers
Michael Chang Winterberg
and Claus Collstrup

design company
Pacesetters

photographers
Charlotte Lassen and
Steffen T. Nielsen

illustrator
Michael Chang Winterberg

country of origin
Denmark

description
A magazine for a co-operative of
four opticians containing articles,
poetry, recipes, and an analysis of
consumer behavior.

dimensions
Spread:
434 x 305 mm
17¹/₈ x 12 in

ABCDEFGHIJKLMNOPQRST

pacesetter

MOD OG ETIK ER IKKE SOFTWARE

Hvorfor bruge den samme typografi til syv forskellige kunder,
når mulighederne for at designe skrifter er grænseløse?
Hvor mange af dine tryksager er typograferet med...

artwork title
Stop

typefaces
Pace In Love, Pace Two,
Pace Helvetica, and Pace Impact

designers
Michael Chang Winterberg
and Claus Collstrup

design company
Pacesetters

country of origin
Denmark

description
A promotional brochure for
Pacesetters, describing their design
philosophy and working methods.

dimensions
Spread:
594 x 210 mm
23³/₈ x 8¹/₄ in

typeface
Pace In Love Regular

typeface family
Pace In Love

designer
Michael Chang Winterberg

foundry/supplier
Pacesetters

country of origin
Denmark

Computer-teknologien er et fantastisk værktøj for den grafiske branche, hvorfor alle reklamebureauer har investeret sig snævertsynede i computere.

Men ideer og identitet forstærkes ikke i takt med at computerne bliver større og bedre, tværtimod!

Computerne er fyldt med de samme programmer, de samme skrifter og de samme muligheder. Det bliver derfor sværere og sværere for bureauer med samme faglige baggrund at skabe et originalt udtryk.

Umiddelbart kan man ikke se på tryksager, hvem afsenderen er, da de er fra reklamebureauernes side er blevet designet med livrem og seler... standard skrifter, standard kreativitet, firkantede billeder, firkantet tankegang.

"VI HAR EN STÆRK IDENTITET!"

Kast et blik på dine foldere.
Forestil dig konkurrentens logo nederst i højre hjørne, og sig højt for dig selv:
Hvorfor investere i en kønsløs, allerede eksisterende identitet?

Eurostile
Helvetica
Garamond
Century Old Style
Futura
Univers
Frutiger
Times

abcdefghijklmnopqrstuvwxyz
1234567890!@&()"?

1234567890!&*(

f

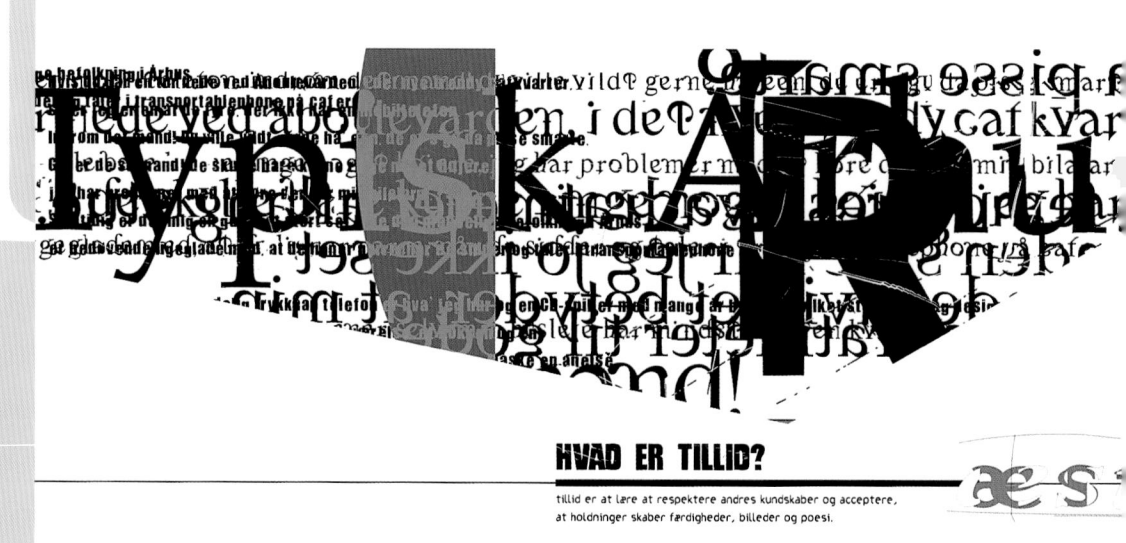

HVAD ER TILLID?

tillid er at lære at respektere andres kundskaber og acceptere,
at holdninger skaber færdigheder, billeder og poesi.

abcdefghijklmnopqrstuv

ABCDEFGHIJKLMNOPQRSTU

artwork title
Stop

typefaces
Pace In Love and Pace Two

designers
Michael Chang Winterberg
and Claus Collstrup

design company
Pacesetters

country of origin
Denmark

description
as on previous spread

dimensions
Spread:
594 x 210 mm
$23^3/_8$ x $8^1/_4$ in

VAD ER TYPOGRAFI?
er at synliggøre ordene mellem linierne.
er korrekt formidlet arkitektonisk kommunikation.
er en kreativ fortolkning af ord.

VAD ER GRAFISK DESIGN?
er en visuel understregning af holdninger og attitude.
er en grafisk profilering af en identitet.
er en æstetisk forførelse af øjet, som fremprovokerer følelser.

pacetters

HVAD ER IDENTITET?
Holdninger, attitude og visualitet.
Pacesetters skaber association til kunst og grafisk poesi. Vi kommunikerer
holdninger og attitude, der ikke forveksles grafisk med noget allerede
eksisterende. typografier designes in-house fra scratch og sælges kun een gang.
Vi har ikke lagt os fast på et grafisk mønster, som siges at have solgt for
milliarder i tidens løb. En kliché der må stamme fra reklamefolk, som tror at
deres fortænkte påfund styrer alt og alle. Vi mener at majonetdukkerne
er i stand til at tænke selv. Pacesetters tillægger ikke markedsføring disse
overnaturlige egenskaber, men revurderer kritisk ordene design, mod og
æstetik, for at skabe et individuelt & solitært image-design, der kommunikerer
holdninger. Vi bliver ikke betalt for at sælge Dem og Deres konkurrenter,
ensartede standardløsninger med ensartede tomme løfter om øget salg.

typeface

Pace Two Black

typeface family
Pace Two

designer
Michael Chang Winterberg

foundry/supplier
Pacesetters

country of origin
Denmark

ABCDEFGHIJKL

artwork title
Stephanie Johnston

typeface
Decibell

designer
Michael Faulkner

design company
RawPaw Graphics

country of origin
UK

description
Cover designs for a record
by Stephanie Johnston

dimensions
305 x 305 mm
12 x 12 in

MNOPQRSTUVWXYZ

1234567890!&·()"?

typeface

Decibell

typeface family
Decibell

designer
Michael Faulkner

foundry/supplier
RawPaw Graphics

country of origin
UK

typeface

Splat

typeface family
Splat

designer
Garry Waller

foundry/supplier
Garry Waller

country of origin
UK

abcdefghijklmn
opqrstuvwxyz
1234567890
?!£%&

ABCDEFGHIJKLMNOPQRSTUVWXYZ

artwork title
Animation Stills

typeface
Splat

designer
Garry Waller

design company
Garry Waller

country of origin
UK

description
The use of the Splat typeface in these animation stills illustrates the gestural and expressive qualities of everyday speech in a conversation between two women.

dimensions
640 x 480 pixels

89

artwork title
Cat Woman Is a Cat Vampire

typeface
Cat Woman

designer
John Wiese

design company
John Wiese

country of origin
USA

description
The designer created the Cat Woman typefaces specifically for the record sleeve and packaging of his experimental noise record.

dimensions
184 x 184 mm
7^1/$_4$ x 7^1/$_4$ in

ABCDEFGHIJKLMNOPQRSTUVWXYZ
1234567890 !&*()"?

ABCDEFGHIJKLMNOPQRSTUVWXYZ
1234567890 !&＊()"?

typefaces

▲Cat Woman–X

◄Cat Woman–Y

typeface family
Cat Woman

designer
John Wiese

foundry/supplier
Prototype Experimental Foundry

country of origin
USA

ABCDEFGHIJKLMNOPQRSTUVWXYZ

artwork title
Caitanya Pranam

typeface
Caitanya

designer
John Wiese

design company
John Wiese

country of origin
USA

description
Poster

dimensions
170 x 278 mm
6³/₄ x 11 in

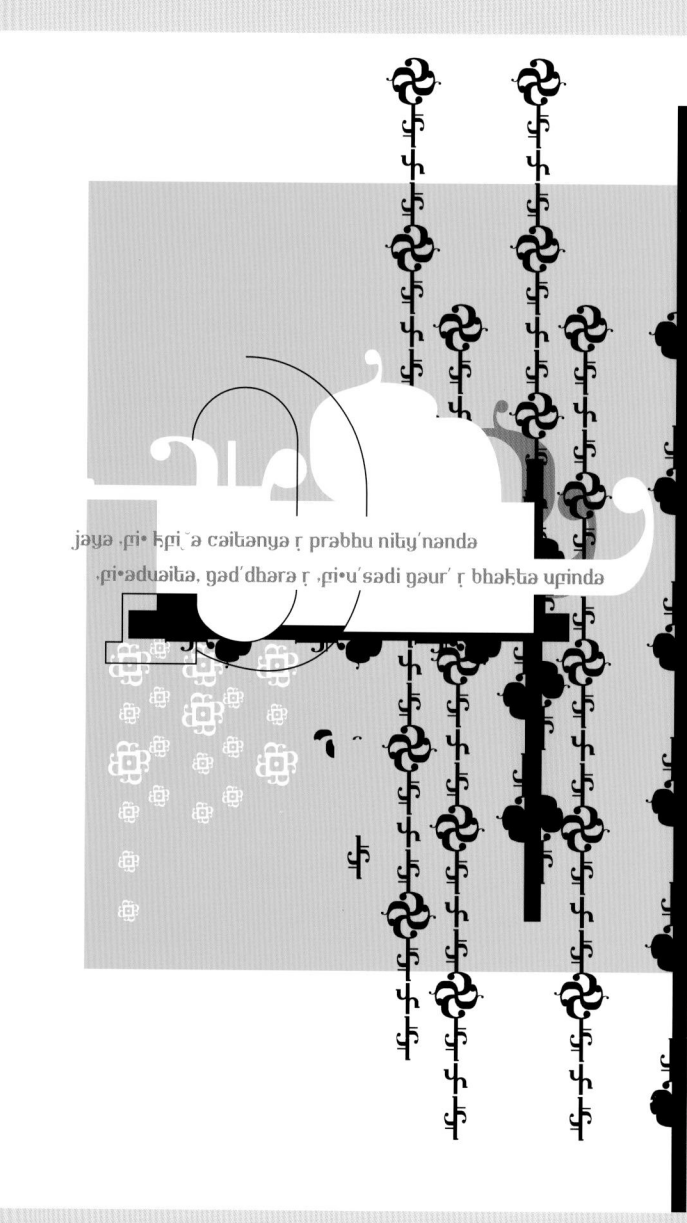

12345
67890
&*"?@

abcde
fghijkl
mnopq
rstuuu
wxyz

typeface

Caitanya Regular

typeface family
Caitanya

designer
John Wiese

foundry/supplier
Prototype Experimental Foundry

country of origin
USA

alpha 2

text and display faces

This section highlights bold new text faces, which also work as display faces.

A B C D E F G H I J K L M N O P Q R S T U V W X Y Z

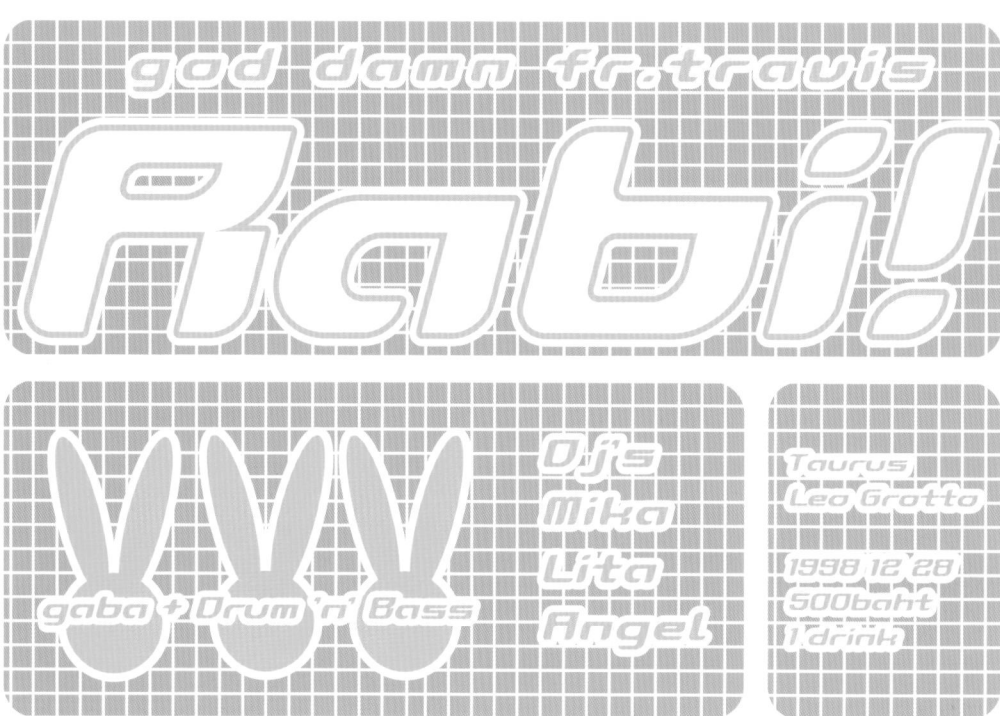

artwork title
Rabi!

typeface
Shark

designer
Atsushi Aoki

design company
Atsushi Aoki

illustrator
Atsushi Aoki

country of origin
Japan

description
Club flyer

dimensions
144 x 97 mm
$5^5/_8$ x $3^7/_8$ in

1234567890

!@&()?

typeface
Shark

typeface family
Shark

designer
Atsushi Aoki

foundry/supplier
Atsushi Aoki

country of origin
Japan

abcdefghi

jklmnopqr

stuvwxyz

ABCDEFGHIJKLMN

OPQRSTUVWXYZ

&()

1234567890

typeface
Holyoke

typeface family
Holyoke

designer
Ann Holyoke Lehmann

foundry/supplier
not available for commercial use

country of origin
USA/Germany

artwork titles
Top right:
The New York School 3
Bottom right:
Karlheinz Stockhausen: Spiral

typeface
Holyoke

designer
Ann Holyoke Lehmann

design company
Ann Holyoke Lehmann

photographer
Ann Holyoke Lehmann

country of origin
Germany/Switzerland

description
CD covers and booklets

dimensions
243 x 120 mm
$9^{5}/_{8}$ x $4^{3}/_{4}$ in

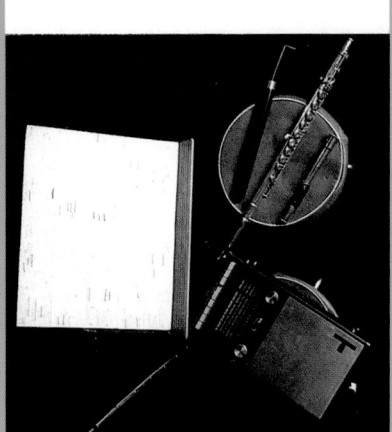

abcdefghijklmnopqrstuvwxyz
1234567890!@&*()"?

ABCDEFGHIJ

NOPQRSTUV

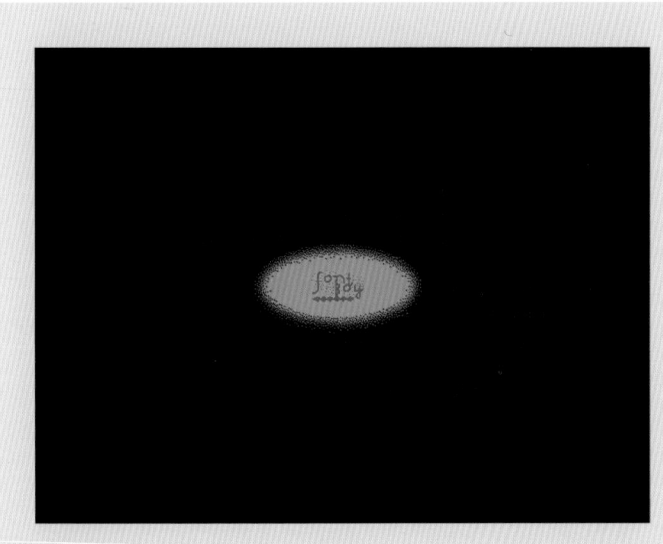

typeface
Armature Bold

typeface family
Armature

designer
Bob Aufuldish

foundry/supplier
fontBoy

country of origin
USA

KLM

WXYZ

artwork title
fontBoy Screensaver

typefaces
all fontBoy fonts

designer
Bob Aufuldish

design company
Aufuldish & Warinner

writer
Mark Bartlett

programming
David Karam and
Dave Granvold

country of origin
USA

description
The fontBoy screensaver uses quotes from Mark Bartlett's essay, "Beyond the Margins of the Page," juxtaposed with a soundtrack of snoring. It connects nine quotations randomly with seven typefaces (two of which are illegible), and then selects a combination to show on-screen. The quotations, which comment on the cultural significance of graphic design, offer a marked contrast to the mundane activity of work.
(See also pages 12–13)

dimensions
640 x 480 pixels

Every word is an em
y vessel
perfectly general
free from all partic
arity
the perfect project
screen that takes on any
degree of specificity

1234567890!@&()"?

abcde
fghijklm
nopqrstu
vwxyz

artwork title
Satellite

typeface
AF Carplates Bold

art director
Christian Küsters

designers
Christian Küsters and Andy Long

design company
CHK Design Ltd.

photographer
Angela Bullock

country of origin
UK

description
Two section dividers from the
book *Satellite* by Angela Bullock.

dimensions
400 x 250 mm
15³/₄ x 9⁷/₈ in

typeface
AF Carplates Bold

typeface family
AF Carplates

designers
Sandy Suffield and Christian Küsters

foundry/supplier
ACME fonts

country of origin
UK

ABCDE
FGHIJK
LMNOP
QRSTU
VWXYZ

BEHAVIOUR

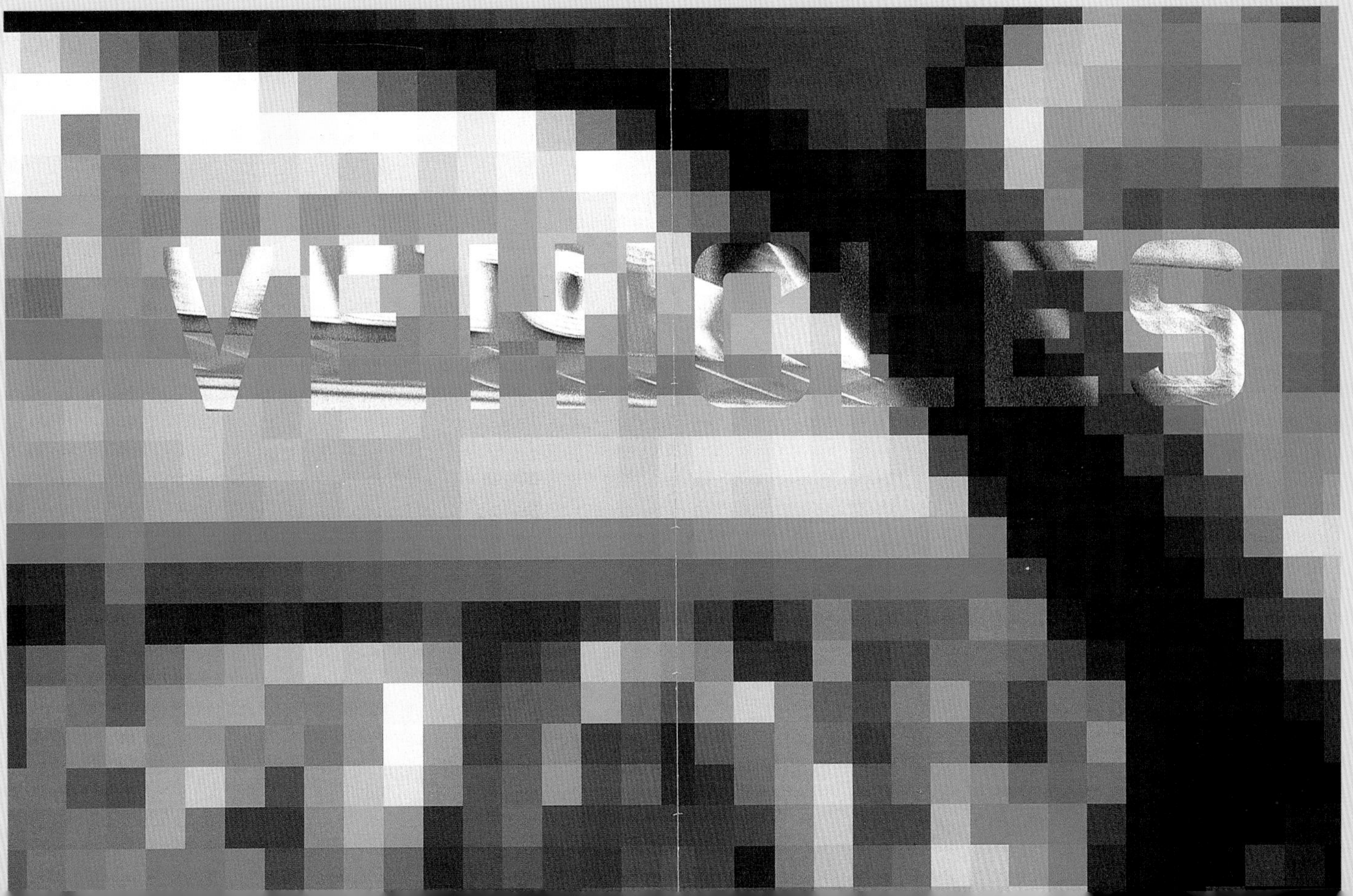
VEHICLES

1234567890!@&*[]?

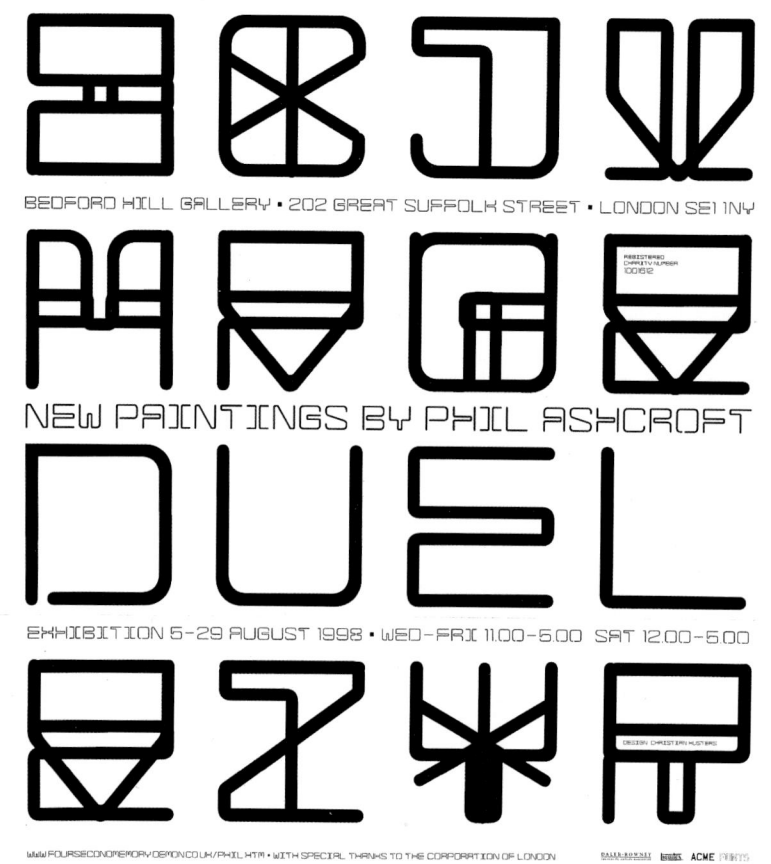

artwork title
Duel

typeface
AF Angel

designer
Christian Küsters

design company
CHK Design Ltd.

country of origin
UK

description
Poster for an exhibition of
paintings by Phil Ashcroft

dimensions
1008 x 1000 mm
39³/₄ x 39³/₈ in

ABCDEFGHI
JKLMNOPQR
STUVWXYZ

typeface

AF Angel Regular

typeface family
AF Angel

designer
Christian Küsters

foundry/supplier
ACME Fonts

country of origin
UK

1234567890!@&*()"?

typeface

AF Hadrian Roman

typeface family
AF Hadrian

designer
Christian Küsters

foundry/supplier
ACME fonts

country of origin
UK

ABCDEFG
HIJKLMNOPQR
STUVWXYZ

Celebrating
the legacy
of two of this
century's
most
inspirational
artistic
figures,
ANTONIN ARTAUD
and JEAN GENET

INCARCERATED with ARTAUD & GENET | 31 May - 2 June

a three day
encounter
including
speakers and
performers
influenced
by their
revolutionary
cultural
vision.

ICA TALKS

artwork title
Incarcerated with Artaud & Genet

typeface
AF Hadrian

designer
Christian Küsters

design company
CHK Design Ltd.

photographer
Christian Küsters

country of origin
UK

description
A promotional card for "Incarcerated with Artaud and Genet"—an event held over three days at the Institute of Contemporary Arts, London, to celebrate the centenary of Artaud's birth and the tenth anniversary of Genet's death.

dimensions
212 x 129 mm
$8^3/_8$ x $5^1/_8$ in

abcdefghijklm
nopqrstuvwxyz

typeface
Son Regular

typeface family
Son

designer
Pascal Béjean

design advisors
Susan LaPorte, Doug Kisor,
and Brian Schorn

foundry/supplier
bulldozer®editions

country of origin
France

abcdefghijklmno
pqrstuvwxyz
1234567890!@()"?
ABCDEFGHIJKLMNO
PQRSTUVWXYZ

artwork title
À Chaque Jour Suffit sa Peine

typeface
Son

designer
Pascal Béjean

design company
bulldozer®editions

country of origin
France

description
An excerpt from P.A.R.T.O.U.Z.E.,
a collective project about intimacy,
organized by bulldozer®editions,
and exhibited in 1997 in the
Gallery 90° in Bordeaux, France.

dimensions
1200 x 1200 mm
47$^1/_4$ x 47$^1/_4$ in

Je joue avec Léonard dans le jardin, lui fais visiter le potager. On s'amuse à sentir les fleurs et la menthe fraîche, le soleil cogne, j'ai du mal à lire le stock de Monde qui traîne au 55 - un jour sans angoisse apparente et pourtant je me sens fragile, l'idée même d'accompagner Léonard à la clinique m'est insupportable - j'ai peur. 4/6/96. _ La clinique : Léonard est en nous, D. résiste, elle est merveilleuse / je l'aime, des coups dans le ventre, je serre les dents, je ne suis pas prêt - c'est ma vie demain qui rentre au bloc.

je brûlerais toutes mes peintures et je signerais un contrat de 10 ans à la SNCF pour que tout se passe bien.

Je ronge mon frein, peut-être m'abrutir sur Doom - Léonard love 5/6/96. _ Vidé. Léonard se remet dans une chaleur étouffante (comme pour sa naissance, il a presque un an - une centaine de degrés) journées longues, il commence à se relever, l'opération est derrière nous, comme un mauvais rêve. J'ai eu peur. J'ai tenu le choc, bien mieux que moi, on ne se refait pas. Léonard se précipite dans nos bras, les yeux voilés et il vogue en nage, il a besoin de nous, on est là. 7/6/96. _ Je n'en peux plus. 11/6/96. _

Léonard est allé rendre visite à ses copains de crèche et il va mieux, il marche presque et pour la première fois il frappe dans ses mains. 13/6/96. _ D. me téléphone.

Léonard a fait cinq pas, les premiers. Je rentre tard, il est couché. 21/6/96. _ Orly 16h45, dans la cohue, valises bouclées in extremis, sans pensée. Léonard prend l'avion pour la première fois, je reste à quai. tte/7/96. _ J'aimerais que D. soit là, entendre L. La vie me semble tout à coup si précieuse et fragile que j'ai envie d'aller vers eux. De la tristesse. Heureusement je sors ce soir, j'aurais eu du mal à rester seul, à m'affronter dans ces moments-là. Je suis lâche. 6/7/96. _ 21h : aéroport, l'avion a du retard et je tourne en rond. L'émotion est forte - je la maîtrise mal, elle me bloque même. Je me sens un peu décalé, gauche. L'esprit en paix

et plein de bonnes résolutions, j'ai envie que la petite famille s'éclate. Léonard a grandi. On s'ouvre une petite bouteille de vin et plein les mains. je file à vélo dans Paris ensoleillé, les courbatures sur le porte-bagages -

plus vite. Léonard dit "Papa" et se précipite dans mes bras. Un bain avec les jouets en plastique, je me rase, il dort. 16/9/96. _

Je speede dans la côte rue de Tolbiac

et retrouve Léonard et Delphine, en nage, je plonge dans le reste de son bain et nous fêtons nos retrouvailles.

A chaque jour suffit sa peine.

Je chante une comptine bien à moi pour l'endormir, j'espère que je ne dérègle pas trop son sens de la mélodie. 23/9/96.

1234567890!@&*()"?

abcde
fghijklmn
opqrstuv
wxyz

ABCDEFGHIJKLMNOPQRSTUVWXYZ

typeface

TableManners
Regular

typeface family
TableManners

designer
Bob Beck

foundry/supplier
Psy/Ops Type Foundry

country of origin
USA

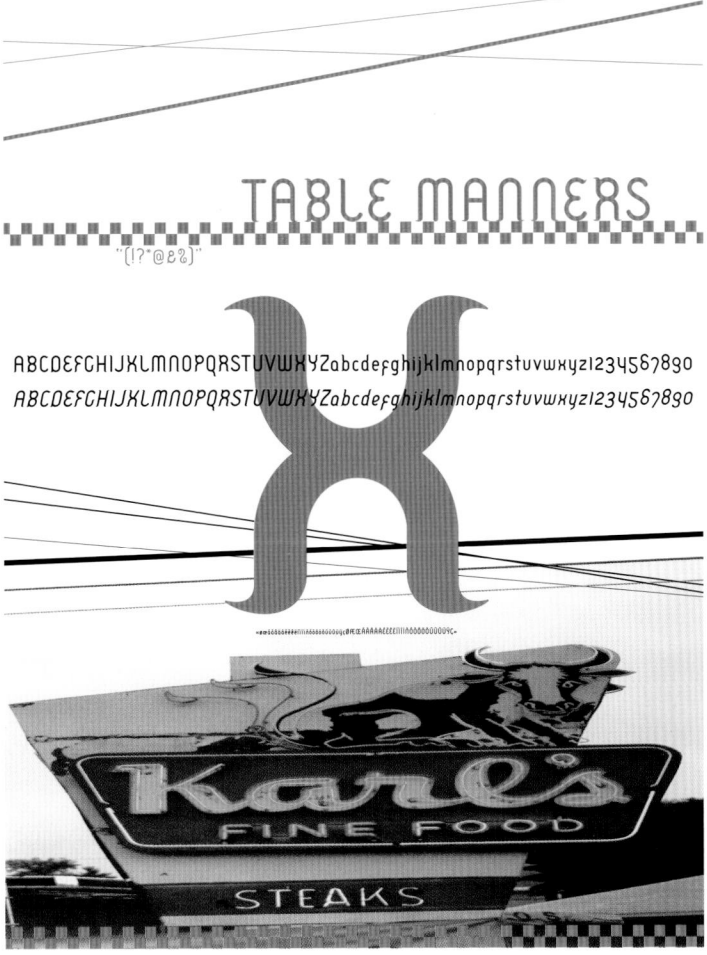

artwork title
TableManners

typefaces
TableManners Regular and
TableManners Italic

designer
Bob Beck

design company
Dialekt

photographer
Bob Beck

country of origin
USA

description
Poster to promote the release
of the TableManners typefaces

dimensions
610 x 813 mm
24 x 32 in

ABCDEFGHIJKLMNOPQRSTUVWXYZ

abcde
fghijklm
nopqrstuvwxyz
1234567890

„Knåggen"
Leitfaden zur Wasagung nach
Art des traditionellen
norwegischen Honsenfestes.

Gesammelt und zeitgemäß
übertragen durch die
hg albrecht werbeagentur.

typeface

bf_BiaBia

typeface family
bf_BiaBia

designer
Guido Schneider

foundry/supplier
brass_fonts cologne

country of origin
Germany

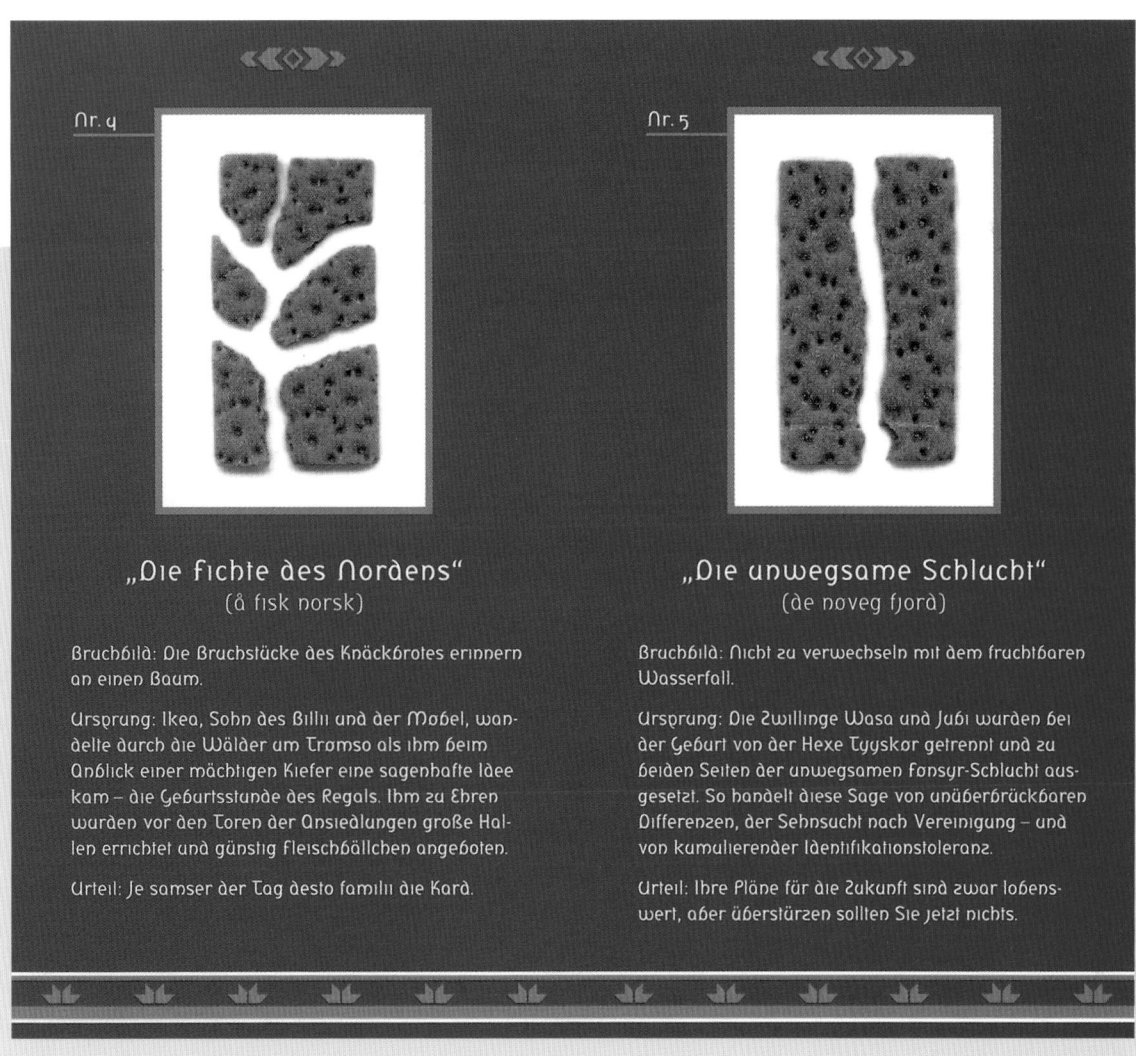

Nr. 4

„Die fichte des Nordens"
(å fisk norsk)

Bruchbild: Die Bruchstücke des Knäckbrotes erinnern an einen Baum.

Ursprung: Ikea, Sohn des Billii und der Mobel, wandelte durch die Wälder um Tromso als ihm beim Anblick einer mächtigen Kiefer eine sagenhafte Idee kam – die Geburtsstunde des Regals. Ihm zu Ehren wurden vor den Toren der Ansiedlungen große Hallen errichtet und günstig Fleischbällchen angeboten.

Urteil: Je samser der Tag desto familii die Kard.

Nr. 5

„Die unwegsame Schlucht"
(de noveg fjord)

Bruchbild: Nicht zu verwechseln mit dem fruchtbaren Wasserfall.

Ursprung: Die Zwillinge Wasa und Jubi wurden bei der Geburt von der Hexe Tyyskor getrennt und zu beiden Seiten der unwegsamen Fansyr-Schlucht ausgesetzt. So handelt diese Sage von unüberbrückbaren Differenzen, der Sehnsucht nach Vereinigung – und von kumulierender Identifikationstoleranz.

Urteil: Ihre Pläne für die Zukunft sind zwar lobenswert, aber überstürzen sollten Sie jetzt nichts.

---

artwork title
Hønsenfest

typeface
bf_BiaBia

designer
Rolf Zaremba

design company
HP Albrecht Advertising Agency

text
Peter Hofmann

illustrator
Rolf Zaremba

country of origin
Germany

description
An invitation, in booklet form, for the opening of the HP Albrecht Advertising Agency's new office on November 20 1998—the Norwegian New Year's Day. The booklet features several ways to tell fortunes and to make predictions for the coming year.

dimensions
cover: 77 x 135 mm, 3 x 5^1/$_4$ in
spread: 154 x 135 mm, 6 x 5^1/$_4$ in

artwork title	illustrator
Medical-Shop Online	René Tillmann

typeface	country of origin
bf_Veto	Germany

art director	description
Martin Bauermeister	The homepage for an internet website selling medical equipment.

designers	
Martin Bauermeister and René Tillmann	dimensions
	640 x 480 pixels

design company
godz advertising_cologne

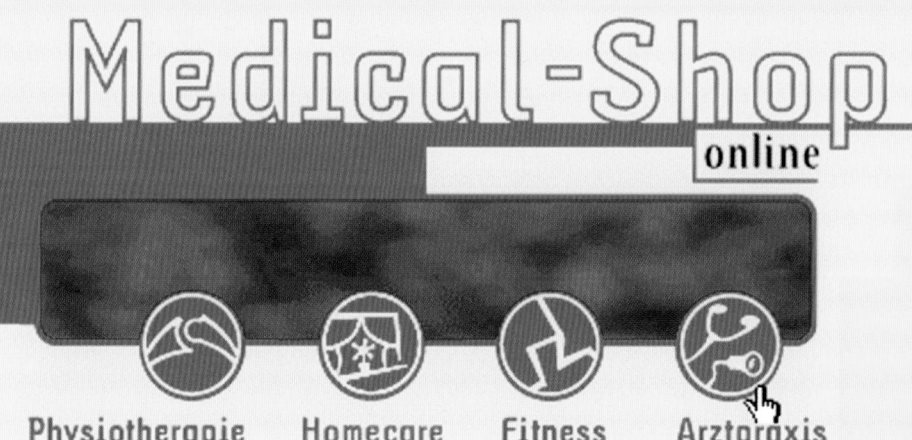

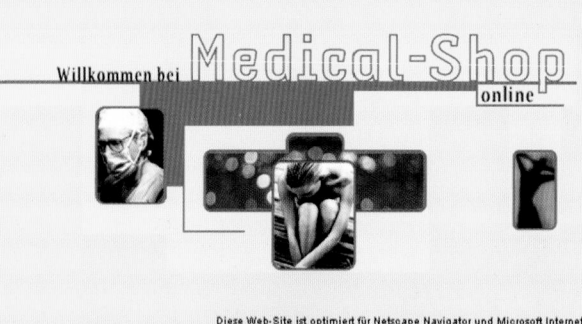

1234567890

ABCDEFG
HIJKLMNOP
QRSTUVWXYZ

!@&*()"?

pqrstuvwxyz

defghijklmno

typeface
bf_Veto Regular

typeface family
bf_Veto

designer
Hartmut Schaarschmidt

foundry/supplier
brass_fonts cologne

country of origin
Germany

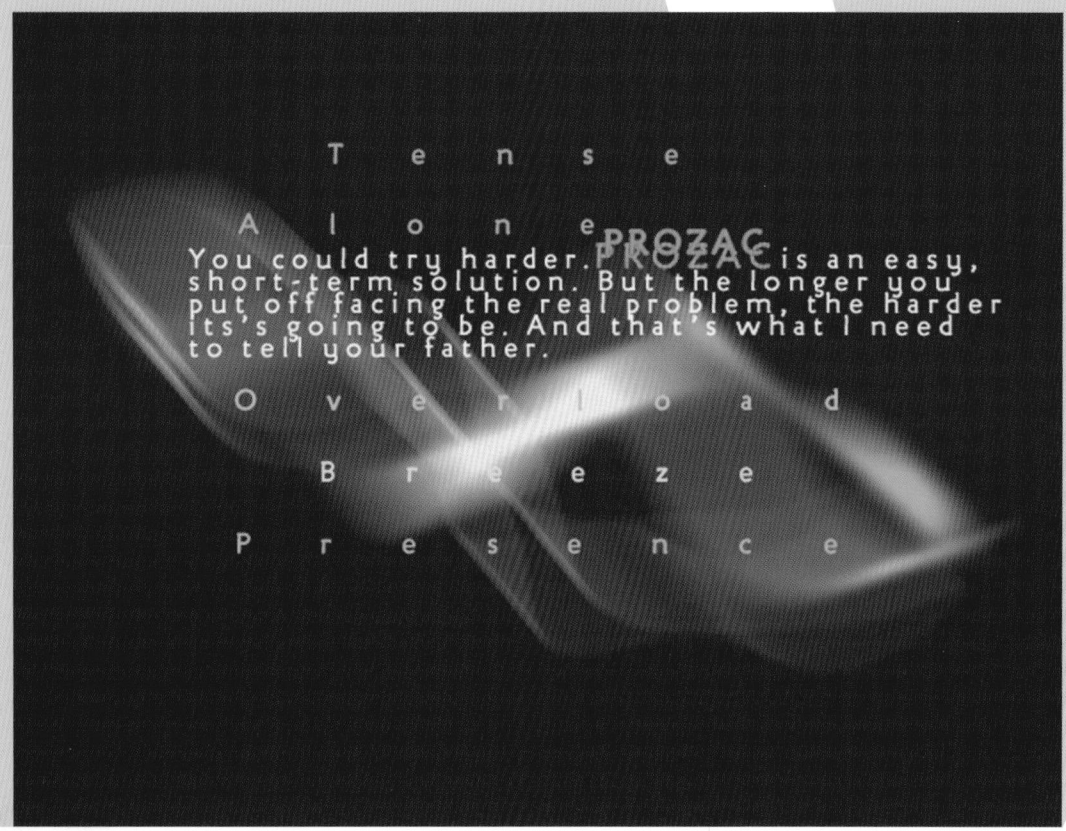

artwork title
The Visitor: Mediadome

typeface
Engine

art director
Ken Olling

designer
Dave Bravenec

design company
Tag Media

illustrator
Dave Bravenec

country of origin
USA

description
A still from a linear, interactive narrative exploring the subconscious of an individual with extraordinary powers.

dimensions
640 x 480 pixels

abcdefghijklm

1234567890!@&*()"?

ABCDEF
GHIJKLMNOPQ
RSTUVWXYZ

typeface
Engine Regular

typeface family
Engine

designer
Alex Scholing

foundry/supplier
FontShop International

country of origin
Germany

nopqrstuvwxyz

abcdefghijklmnopqrstuvwxyz

1234567890!&*()"?

ABCDEFGHIJKLMNOPQRSTUVWXYZ

typeface
BD Globus

typeface family
BD Globus

designer
H1reber

foundry/supplier
büro destruct

country of origin
Switzerland

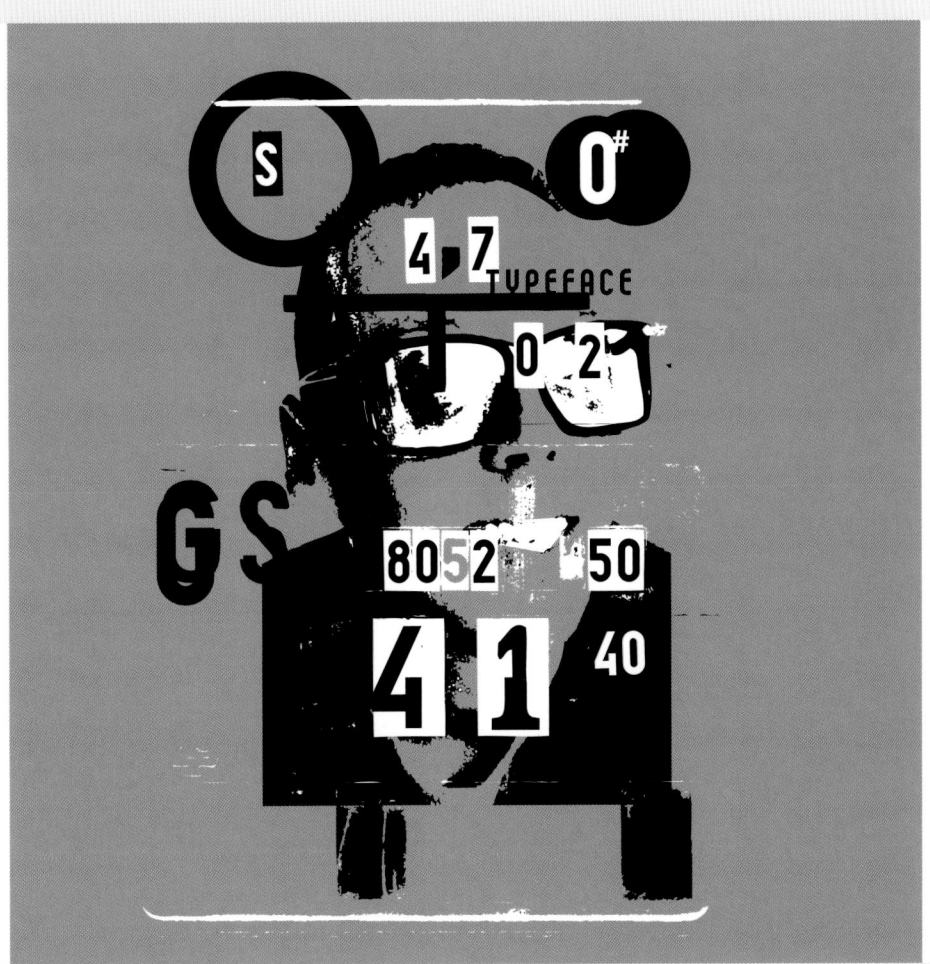

artwork title
TypeFace#1

typeface
BD Globus

art director
H1reber

designer
MBrunner

design company
büro destruct

country of origin
Switzerland

description
Image from the büro destruct
TypeFace exhibition

dimensions
1000 x 1000 mm
$39^3/_8$ x $39^3/_8$ in

typeface
phliteAudrey

typeface family
phliteAudrey

designer
Hwee Min Loi

foundry/supplier
Hwee Min Loi

country of origin
USA

ABCDEFGHIJKLMNOPQRSTUUWXYZ

abcde
fghijklm
nopqrs
tuvwxyz

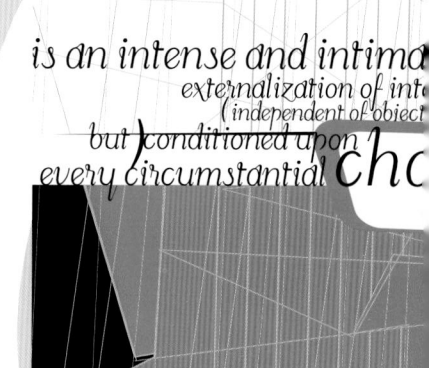

is an intense and intima
externalization of inte
(independent of object
but)conditioned upon
every circumstantial cho

Beauty

red experiences,
cism

ge in the before, during and after...

(s)

artwork title
On Beauty

typeface
phliteAudrey

designer
Hwee Min Loi

college
California Institute of the Arts

illustrator
Hwee Min Loi

country of origin
USA

description
Taken from a graduate thesis
exploring the concept of beauty,
this poster is the last in a series of
six. The work seeks to redefine the
meaning of beauty according to
the results of the student's research
into its cultural significance.

dimensions
1219 x 813 mm
48 x 32 in

Mercury™ Regular

typeface family
Mercury

designer
Peter Bruhn

foundry/supplier
Fountain

country of origin
Sweden

artwork title
Mercury Promotion

typeface
Mercury

designer
Peter Bruhn

design company
Fountain

photographer
Peter Bruhn

country of origin
Sweden

description
Promotional images for
the Mercury typeface

dimensions
123 x 138 mm
$4^7/_8$ x $5^1/_2$ in

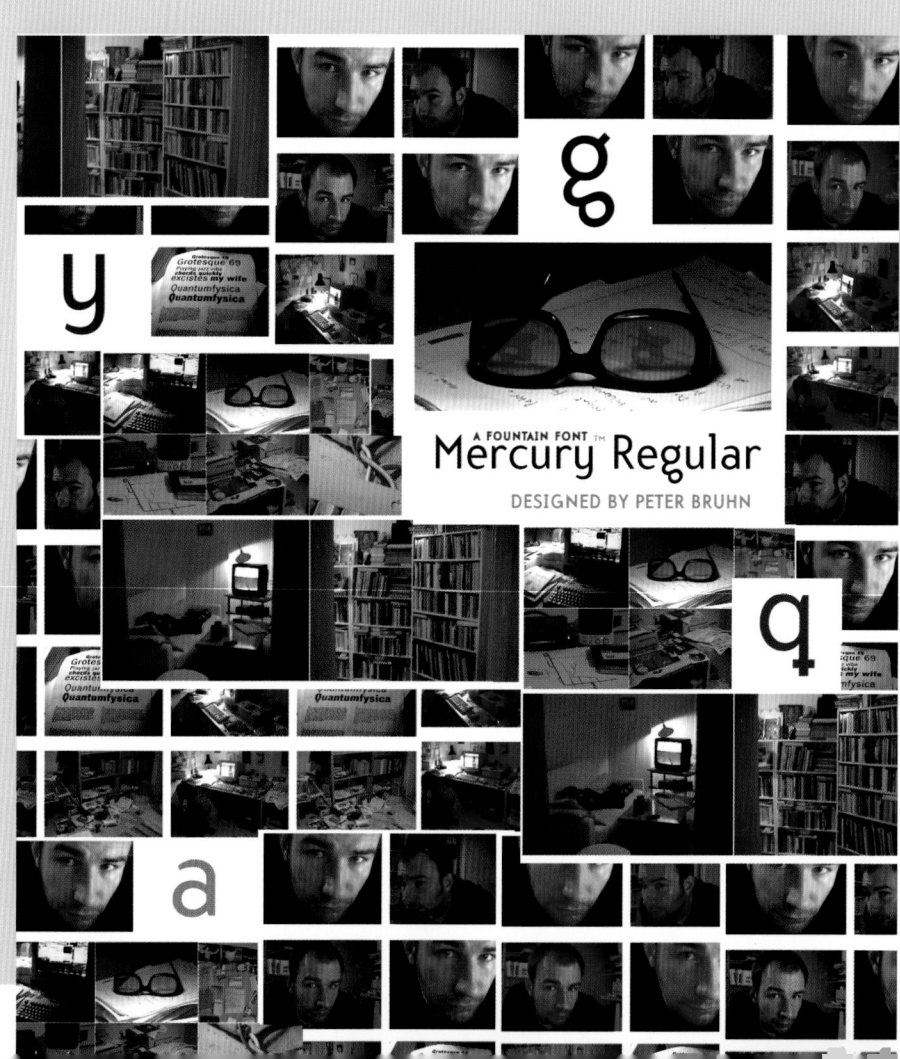

a genuine fountain font

mercury designed by

peter bruhn

lagom tuff!

a family of

10

abcdefghijklmnopqrstuvwxyz

1234567890!@&*()"?

ABCDEFGHIJKLMNOPQRSTUVWXYZ

ABCDEFGHIJKLMNOPQRS

abcdefghijk lmnop qrstu vwxyz

typeface
Theodor

typeface family
Theodor

designer
Peter Bruhn

foundry/supplier
Fountain

country of origin
Sweden

1234567890!@&

TUVWXYZ

artwork title
Theodor Promotion

typeface
Theodor

designer
Peter Bruhn

design company
Fountain

country of origin
Sweden

description
Promotional image for
the Theodor typeface

dimensions
160 x 120 mm
6¹/₄ x 4³/₄ in

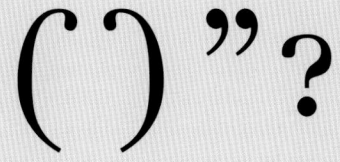

abcdefGHijklm
NOPQRStUVWXYZ

123
4567
890!
@G*()
"?

typeface
Gas™

typeface family
Gas

designer
Peter Bruhn

foundry/supplier
Fountain

country of origin
Sweden

ABCDEFGHIJKLM

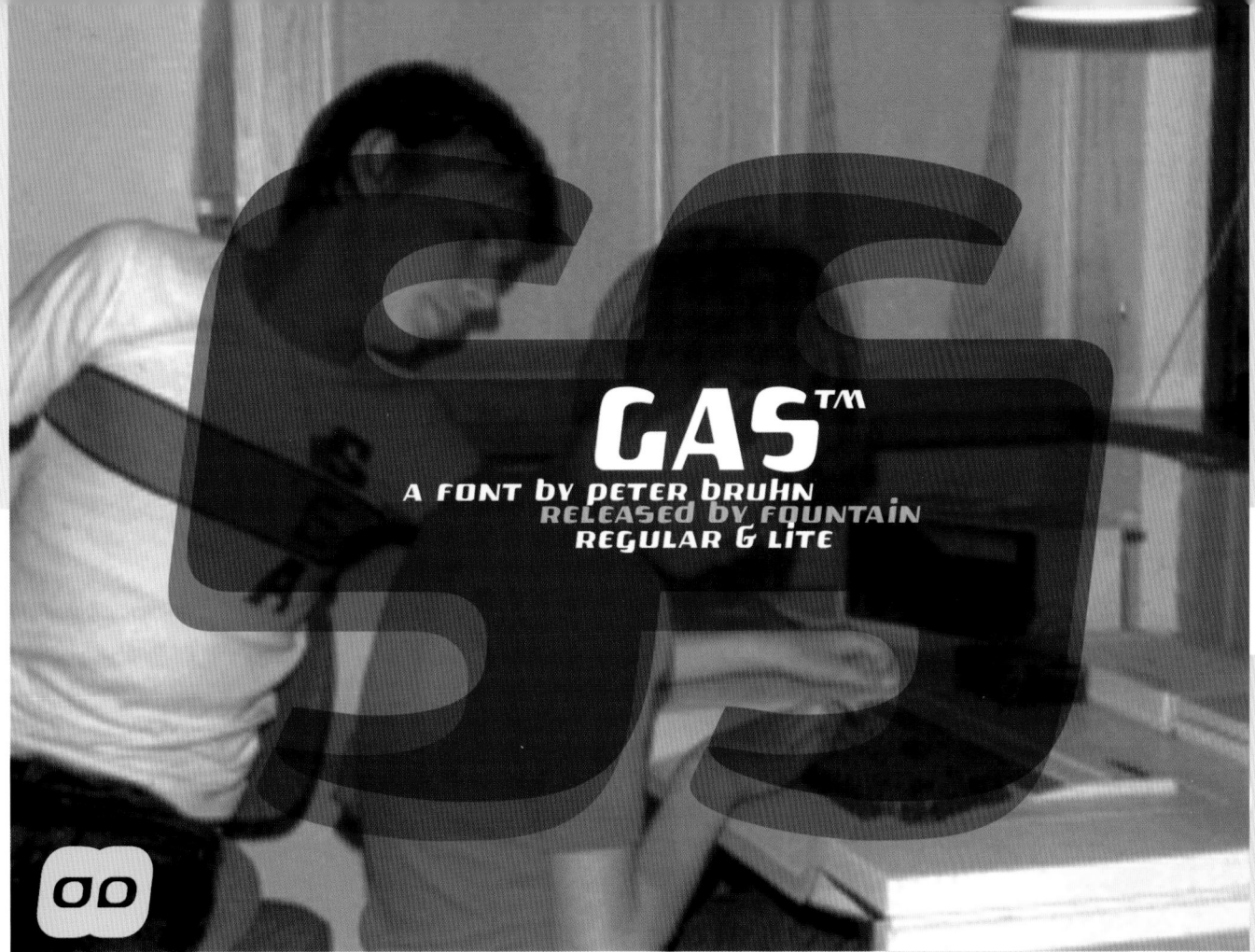

GAS™
A FONT BY PETER BRUHN
RELEASED BY FOUNTAIN
REGULAR & LITE

artwork title
Gas Promotion

typeface
Gas

designer
Peter Bruhn

design company
Fountain

photographer
Wolfgang Bruhn

country of origin
Sweden

description
Promotional image
for the Gas typeface

dimensions
160 x 120 mm
6^1/$_4$ x 4^3/$_4$ in

NOPQRSTUVWXYZ

typeface

Shiretype Shropshire

typeface family
The Shire Types

designer
Jeremy Tankard

foundry/supplier
Jeremy Tankard | Typography

country of origin
UK

artwork title
The Shire Types Promotion

typefaces
The Shire Types and Bliss

designer
Jeremy Tankard

design company
Jeremy Tankard | Typography

country of origin
UK

description
A promotional poster demonstrating the full range of typefaces in the Shire Types family. It also gives information on the concepts behind their creation.

dimensions
410 x 544 mm
16¼ x 21³/₈ in

SHIRETYPE CHESHIRE
abcdefghijklmnopqrstuvwxyz
1234567890!@&*()"?

SHIRETYPE DERBYSHIRE
ABCDEFGHIJKLMNOPQRSTUVWXYZ
1234567890!@&*()"?

SHIRETYPE STAFFORDSHIRE
ABCDEFGHIJKLMNOPQRSTUVWXYZ
1234567890!@&*()"?

Shiretype warwickshire
abcdefghijklmnopqrstuvwxyz
1234567890!@&*()"?

Shiretype worcestershire
abcdefghijklmnopqrstuvwxyz
1234567890!@&*()"?

1234567890

!@&*()"?

abcdefghijklm
nopqrstuvwxyz

¶ THE LETTER FORMS OF THE SHIRES CHANGE STYLE AS YOU MOVE AROUND THEM AND, LIKE PEOPLE, ARE NOT TIED TO ANY ONE PLACE BUT CAN TRAVEL FREELY FROM SHIRE TO SHIRE AND MIX WITH THEIR NEIGHBOURS.

As the Industrial Revolution gained momentum in the nineteenth century, a need for a strong, brash and aggressive letter form was created. The letter had to shout its presence above that of the well spoken Roman. The resulting letter was not crude and ugly, as often claimed, but exerted new beauty through its proportions and austere authority.

¶ABCDEFGHIJKLŁM
NOPQRSTUVWXYZÞ
FIFL1234567890½¼
¾&ÁÅÇÉÍÑÓØÚÝŸÆŒ
AO™#%$!?¤£€$¢¥ƒ
®©@",.¶ABCDEFG
HIJKLŁMNOPQRSTU
VWXYZÞFIFL123456
7890¾¼ÁÅÇÉÍÑÚÝŸÆ
ŒA™",.ABCDEFGHI
JKLŁMNOPQRSTUVW
XYZFIFLẞ12345678
90&áåçéíñúÿÿÆŒa™
@",.ABCDEFGHIJK
LŁMNOPQRSTUVWX
YZFIFL1234567890
½áåçéíñúÿÆŒa™£"
,.¶ABCDEFGHIJKLŁ
MNOPQRSTUVWXYZ
FIFLẞ1234567890½
¼¾&áåçéíñúÿœÆa
™!?£@",.¶ABCDEFG
HIJKLŁMNOPQRSTU
VWXYZFIFLẞ123456
7890½¼áåçéíñúÿœ
Œa™?£",.-+)}]¹²³●

Derbyshire | Staffordshire | Cheshire | Shropshire | Warwickshire | Worcestershire

The Shire Types™ consist of six typefaces that include all the standard ISO/Adobe characters. The range of characters available depends on the software and hardware platform being used. The types are available for Mac and PC and include the new Euro Currency Symbol €.

Jeremy Tankard | Typography
www.typography.net

Köln
VRÅ
Øster
TRÉS
ÆSTHETIC
ŒDIPUS

There are no ascenders or descenders in The Shire Types, accented characters shrink to fit the general character height and capital letters mix happily with their less stately comrades; it is a classless and caseless system. The resulting word shapes from this linguistic interaction can be very interesting and acceptable, all being hybrids of a familiar face.

AAAaaaaa

Derbyshire | Staffordshire | Cheshire | Shropshire | Warwickshire | Worcestershire

Inspiration for the basic shapes came from the Grotesque and Egyptian lettering styles of the Industrial Revolution. The intent was not to pastiche but to revitalise these forms, which in turn have been blended with a variety of interpretations of the shires; including position, industry, dialect, history and countryside.

DERBYSHIRE
STAFFORDSHIRE
CHESHIRE
SHROPSHIRE
warwickshire
worcestershire

The typefaces take their names from six of the shires that are grouped together around the Black Country and the neighbouring rural areas.

Six typefaces designed to create a dense textural mass of lettering

tw fontWORKS

¶ the shires ARE THE MIDLAND COUNTIES OF ENGLAND.

as the industrial revolution gained momentum in the nineteenth century, a need for a strong, brash and aggressive letter form was created. the letter had to shout its presence above that of the well spoken roman. the resulting letter was not crude and ugly, as often claimed, but exerted a new beauty through its proportions and austere authority.

THE SHIRE TYPES

0171 490 5390

Text type is set in Bliss, for more information contact Jeremy Tankard 0411 589 083
The Shire Types © Jeremy Tankard 1998 · Bliss © Jeremy Tankard 1996

"CONCEIVED WITH PASSION BY UNKNOWN ARTISTS, & CONSUMED IN IMAGE IF NOT IN USAGE BY A WHOLE POPULATION WHICH APPROPRIATES THEM AS A PURELY MAGICAL OBJECT."

The populist interpretation of the Middle Ages is one of magic and mystery. Many bizarre symbol alphabets were developed during this period, from the simplicity of Runes to the very strange Celestial, Alchemical and Slavic alphabets. Elements from these forms have been recreated with those from the Manuscripts resulting in the graphic forms of Alchemy.

some key strokes contain pre-designed ligatures

diamond finials can be attached to either side of a character

the monastic scribes twisted and stretched their illuminated letters into graphic forms of almost infinite variety

superior letters are contained in Alchemy Silver High

The Manuscripts of the Middle Ages contain a rich diversity and ingenious use of capital lettering. During this period the monastic scribes twisted and stretched their illuminated letters into graphic forms of almost infinite variety. Many of the letter forms of the Alchemy typeface have been derived from the decorated pages of the Lindisfarne Gospels (around 698ad), which contain Anglo-Saxon capitals that have several alternative forms and appear freely mixed together to enhance a word's shape.

many bizarre symbol alphabets were developed during the Middle Ages

a linking bar joins characters and continues the line of the diamond finials

inferior letters are contained in Alchemy Silver Low

Plug-in characters allow for the creation of a multitude of ligatures

Alchemy™ is an extended alphabet that consists of four typefaces which include all the standard ISO/Adobe characters. The range of alternative characters available depends on the software and hardware platform being used. The types are available for the Macintosh computer and include the new Euro Currency Symbol €.

Jeremy Tankard | Typography
www.typography.net

A menagerie of letters and ligatures to create detailed and varied word shapes in a modern gothic style

after Roland Barthes 'Mythologies' [1957] 'La Nouvelle Citroën'

The four faces of Alchemy

ALCHEMY GOLD 24
ALCHEMY GOLD 18
SILVER HIGH
SILVER LOW

Alchemy is defined as 'seeking to turn base metals into gold or silver'. This idea has been retained in the naming of the Alchemy types with Gold 24 and Gold 18 containing the main letter forms and Silver High and Silver Low containing superior and inferior letter positions. All key strokes contain a character, some of which are pre-designed ligatures, others have the ability to 'plug-in' to other characters to create new ligatures. There is also a linking bar and diamond finials that can be attached to either side of a letter form.

ALCHEMY

fw

0171 490 5390

Text type is set in Bliss, for more information contact Jeremy Tankard 0411 589 083
Alchemy © Jeremy Tankard 1998 · Bliss © Jeremy Tankard 1996

fontWORKS

ABCDEFGHIJKLMN
OPQRSTUVWXYZ

1234567890!@&*(){}"?

ABCDEFGHIJKLMN
OPQRSTUVWXYZ

ALCHEMY GOLD B18
ABCDEFGHIJKLMNOPQRSTUVWXYZ
ABCDEFGHIJKLMNOPQRSTUVWXYZ
1234567890!@&*(){}"?

ALCHEMY SILVER HIGH
ABCDEFGHIJKLMNOPQRSTUVWXYZ
ABCDEFGHIJKLMNOPQRSTUVWXYZ
1234567890!@&*(){}"?

ALCHEMY SILVER LOW
ABCDEFGHIJKLMNOPQRSTUVWXYZ
ABCDEFGHIJKLMNOPQRSTUVWXYZ
1234567890!@&*(){}"?

typeface

Alchemy Gold A24

typeface family
Alchemy

designer
Jeremy Tankard

foundry/supplier
Jeremy Tankard | Typography

country of origin
UK

artwork title
Alchemy Promotion

typefaces
Alchemy and Bliss

designer
Jeremy Tankard

design company
Jeremy Tankard | Typography

country of origin
UK

description
A promotional poster showing the full character set of Alchemy typefaces. Alchemy was originally commissioned by an advertising agency for use in a poster campaign.

dimensions
410 x 544 mm
16$\frac{1}{4}$ x 21$\frac{3}{8}$ in

artwork title
Cult of Virus Catalog

typeface
Patriot

designer
Jon Barnbrook

design company
FontWorks UK Ltd.

country of origin
UK

description
Booklet of typeface specimens

dimensions
209 x 296 mm
8¹/₄ x 11⁵/₈ in

1234567890!@&*()"?

A B C D E
F G H I J K L
M N O P Q
R S T U
V W X Y Z

typeface
Patriot Heavy

typeface family
Patriot

designer
Jon Barnbrook

foundry/supplier
Virus

country of origin
UK

A B C D E F
G H I J K L M N
⊕ P Q R S +
U V W X Y Z

artwork title
Cult of Virus Catalog

typeface
Nixon Script

designer
Jon Barnbrook

design company
FontWorks UK Ltd.

country of origin
UK

description
as on previous spread

dimensions
209 x 296 mm
8¹/₄ x 11⁵/₈ in

abcdefghijklmnopqrstuvwxyz
1234567890!@&*()"?
ABCDEFGHIJKLMNOPQRSTUVWXYZ

abcdefghijklm

typeface

Nixon Script

typeface family
Nixon

designer
Jon Barnbrook

foundry/supplier
Virus

country of origin
UK

134

This is the typeface to tell lies in

The Two faces of

This is the typeface to invade other countries whose culture you do not understand with. This is the typeface to take over the United Nations with. This is the typeface to ignore human rights abuses in China with. This is the typeface to not have a proper health system with. This is the typeface which allows the gun lobby too much control resulting in thousands of innocent deaths a year with. This is the typeface to talk about the lie of the American dream with.

The Two faces of

Nixon

Nixon

artwork title
Cult of Virus Catalog

typefaces
Nylon and Draylon

designer
Jon Barnbrook

design company
FontWorks UK Ltd.

country of origin
UK

description
as on page 132

dimensions
209 x 296 mm
8¹/₄ x 11⁵/₈ in

typeface

Nylon

typeface family
Nylon

designer
Jon Barnbrook

foundry/supplier
Virus

country of origin
UK

ABCDEFGHIJKLMNOPQR

STUVWXYZ

1234567890!@&*()"?

ABCDEFGHIJKLMNOPQR

STUVWXYZ

typeface

Draylon

typeface family
Draylon

designer
Jon Barnbrook

foundry/supplier
Virus

country of origin
UK

ABCDEFGHIJKLMNOPQR

STUVWXYZ

1234567890!@&*()"?

ABCDEFGHIJKLMNOPQR

STUVWXYZ

artwork title
Fresh Ideas

typeface
Seviche

designer
Gerry Chapleski

design company
Gerry Chapleski Design

country of origin
USA

description
Fresh fruit forms a visual metaphor
on the cover of this brochure
promoting new designs.

dimensions
216 x 216 mm
8^1/$_2$ x 8^1/$_2$ in

ABCDEFGHIJKLMNOPQRSTUVWXYZ

1234567890!@&*()""?

nopst

abcdefghijklmnop
qrstuvwxyz

typeface
Seviche

typeface family
Seviche

designer
Gerry Chapleski

foundry/supplier
Editable Graphics

country of origin
USA

AQUATECH

S Y S T E M S

artwork title
Aquatech logo

typefaces
Seviche and Gill Sans

designer
Gerry Chapleski

design company
Gerry Chapleski Design

illustrator
Gerry Chapleski

country of origin
USA

description
Waves of water form the letter "a,"
which is echoed in the accompanying
typography for this logo designed for
a company that sells and installs
swimming pools.

dimensions
not applicable

ABCDEFG H I J K

abcdefghijkl mnopqrstuvwxyz

typeface

Lagrima

typeface family
Lagrima

designer
Gerry Chapleski

foundry/supplier
Editable Graphics

country of origin
USA

STUVW X

1234567890!@&*()"?

LMN O P Q R

MICHAEL THOMPSON

PRODUCER
855 Pennsylvania St., Suite 405
Denver, CO 80203
303•832•5458

YZ

artwork title
Michael Thompson

typeface
Lagrima

designer
Gerry Chapleski

design company
Gerry Chapleski Design

country of origin
USA

description
The image of a gangster firing a
Thompson machine gun is a visual
pun on the movie producer's name
in this design for his business card.

dimensions
89 x 51 mm
3¹/₂ x 2 in

abcdefghijklmnopqrstuvwxyz
123456789!@&*()"?
ABCDEFGHIJKLMNOPQRSTUVWYZ

typeface

PP Barthes

typeface family
Le Pretension Project™

designer
Jens Gehlhaar

foundry/supplier
Jens Gehlhaar

country of origin
USA

artwork title
A Show of Balinese and
Javanese Music and Dance

typefaces
PP Barthes, Letraset Revue,
and ITC Korinna

designer
Jens Gehlhaar

photographer
Jens Gehlhaar

country of origin
USA

description
A poster for the Indonesian music
program at the California Institute
of the Arts.

dimensions
565 x 762 mm
22$^{1}/_{4}$ x 30 in

MUSIC & DANCE

A SHOW OF *Balinese and Javanese*

I Nyoman Wenten
Pak Djoko Walujo
Nanik Wenten

MUSIC AND DANCE UNDER THE DIRECTION OF

JON PARSONS BFA RECITAL

SUNDAY MAY 4TH 1997 8PM
CALARTS ROOM A114
(THE GAMELAN ROOM)

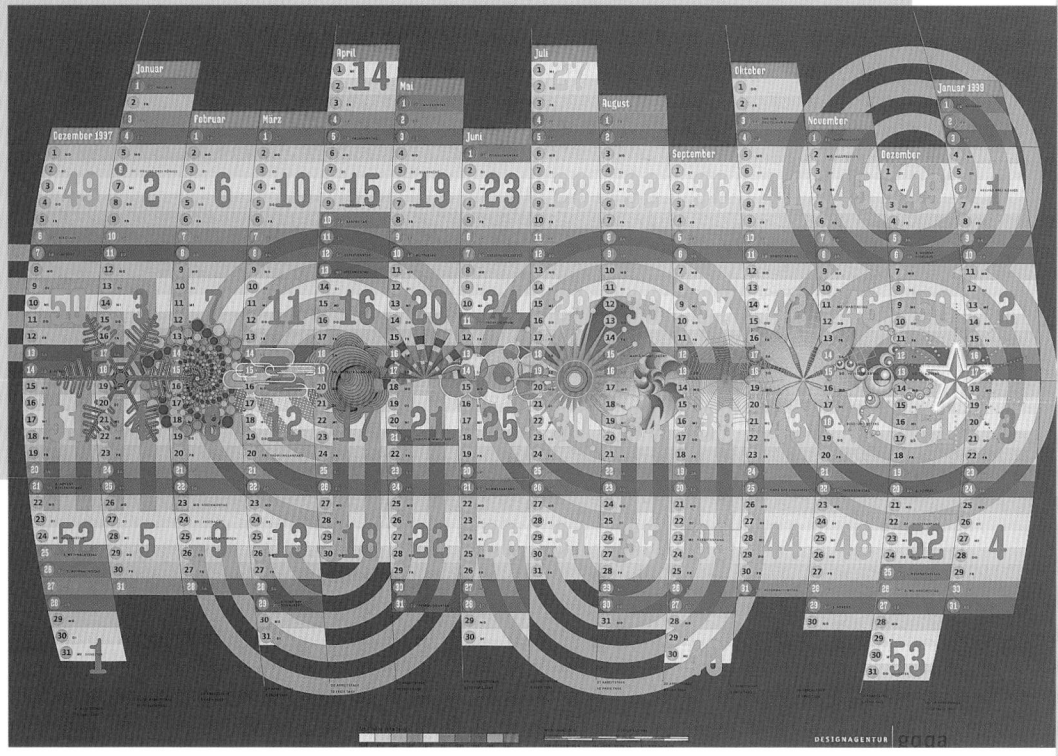

artwork title
Gaga Design Wall Calendar 1998

typefaces
PP Deleuze, PP Lyotard,
and Foundry Journal

designer
Jens Gehlhaar

design company
Gaga Design

illustrator
Jens Gehlhaar

country of origin
USA

description
A wall calendar for German design
studio Gaga Design, created in
1997 to commemorate their 10th
anniversary. The design incorporates
cartographic elements, timezone
graphics, and topographic earth
maps, picking up on the themes of
seasons, climate, leisure, and holidays
to celebrate free time rather than
work days.

dimensions
977 x 679 mm
$38^7/_8$ x $26^3/_4$ in

ab
cdefghijkl
mnopqrs
tuvwx
yz

typeface
PP Deleuze

typeface family
Le Pretension Project™

designer
Jens Gehlhaar

foundry/supplier
Jens Gehlhaar

country of origin
USA

1234567890!@&*()"?
ABCDEFGHIJKLMNOPQRSTUVWXYZ

artwork title
Anne Burdick Presents
Andrew Blauvelt

typefaces
CIA Humdrum and CIA Earthworm

designer
Jens Gehlhaar

design company
Jens Gehlhaar

country of origin
USA

description
This poster was designed for a lecture questioning the relevance of Professor Andrew Blauvelt's academic theorizing. It makes humorous references to Blauvelt's style of writing, which is characterized by a liberal use of slashes, parentheses and lots of footnotes, and it also pokes fun at the visual mannerisms of Cranbrook Academy of Art.

dimensions
502 x 711 mm
19³/₄ x 28 in

abcdefghijklmnopqrstuvwxyz
1234567890!@&*()"?
ABCDEFGHIJKLMNOPQRSTUVWXYZ

typeface

CIA Humdrum

typeface family
The CIA Compendium

designer
Jens Gehlhaar

foundry/supplier
Jens Gehlhaar

country of origin
USA

"You can dance, you can jive
having the time of your life
(Uhuhuh) See that girl, watch that scene
Diggin' the dancing queen"

Ann Burdick presents:

Andrew

Blauvelt:

IMAGE

DESIGN/ENSOGEH/HAAR

RETHINKING
REPACKING,
REMAKING
REDEFINING: 3

1
"Andrew Blauvelt is Director of the
Graduate Program in the Department
of Graphic Design, N.C. State
University, Raleigh. Blauvelt is a
project tutor at the Jan van Eyck
Akademie, Maastricht, the
Netherlands, and a visiting critic in
design history and theory at the newly
established graduate program at the
University of the Americas, Puebla,
Mexico. In 1995/1996 he served as
an Interim Chair of the 2-D Design
Department at Cranbrook Academy
of Art. He is a practicing designer for
cultural and educational clients. The
work for these clients has been widely
exhibited and published including in
Emigre, *Eye*, and *I.D.* magazines as
well as in the ACD, AIGA, TDC NY,
and in the books *The Graphic Edge*
and *Typography Now 2*. He writes
design criticism for *Emigre*, *Eye* and
Design Issues among others, and
recently guest-edited the series, "New
Perspectives: Critical History of
Graphic Design," for the journal
Visible Language as well as "The Info-
Perplex," issue #40, for *Emigre*.
Blauvelt is a board member of the
American Center for Design." 1

The Writing of Cultures of Design and the
Design of Writing of Cultures and the Cultures of Design
of Writing and Writing of Design of Cultures and the
Design of Cultures of Writing and the Cultures
of Writing of Design or: 4

TEXT

B

A: Taken from: "Outside the
Basic Curriculum: Redefining
Education and Artistic
Practice." Conference poster,
designed by Andrew Blauvelt
and Ann Burdick, 1995.

B: Taken from: "Master of
Graphic Design Recruitment."
Poster/brochure, designed by
Andrew Blauvelt, 1995.

C: Taken from: "Remaking
History: the Convergence of
Graphic Design, History,
Theory and Criticism for
Creative Practice." Poster/
program, designed by Andrew
Blauvelt, 1996.

2
"Andrew Blauvelt teaches graduate
studies in the Department of Graphic
Design at the School of Design, North
Carolina State University, Raleigh. He
writes occasionally and lectures
frequently on the social and cultural
condition of graphic design. A
graduate of Cranbrook Academy of
Art, his work produced in the practice
of graphic design has been included
in numerous national and international
design exhibitions and publications.
He is currently interested in the hybrid
forms resulting in the colli/u/sion of
writing and designing practices." 2

3
"Born in 1964, Andrew Blauvelt
received a BFA from Herron School
of Art and an MFA from Cranbrook
Academy of Art. He teaches at North
Carolina State University and in 1995
occupied the interim chair of graphic
design at Cranbrook. As a designer,
he works for cultural and educational
clients. In 1990, his work was exhibited
in the touring exhibition "Cranbrook
Design: the New Discourse" and he
has received recognition in the *I.D.
Annual Design Review*. He edited the
Visible Language series: "New
Perspectives: Critical Histories of
Graphic Design" and writes for *Emigre*
and *Eye*." 3

4
"Andrew Blauvelt leads a hybrid life
in Raleigh, NC, where he is Director
of Graduate Studies in Graphic Design
at NC State University." 4

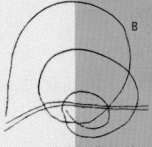

C

ANOTHER
IMAGE

1 : Taken from the biography
section on: Andrew Blauvelt
(des.): "Remaking History: The
Convergence of Graphic
Design, History, Theory, and
Criticism for Creative
Practice." A poster/brochure
for a conference held by the
American Center for Design in
Chicago, Illinois, on February
28, March 1 & 2, 1997.

2: Taken from the biography
section in: Rick Poynor (ed.):
"Typography Now: Implosion,"
p220. Booth-Clibborn
Editions, London, UK, 1996.

3: Taken from the credit
paragraph of: Andrew
Blauvelt: "Unfolding
Information." In: Andrew
Blauvelt (ed.): Emigre #40,
"The Info-Perplex," p27.
Sacramento, CA, 1996.

4: Taken from the biography
section in: Ann Burdick (ed.):
Emigre #35, "Mouthpiece #1,"
p5. Sacramento, CA, 1995.

5: Taken from the credit
paragraph in: Andrew
Blauvelt: "An Opening: Graphic
Design's Discursive Spaces."
In: Andrew Blauvelt (ed.):
"Visible Language 28.3," p205.
Rhodes Island, RI, 1996

5
"Andrew Blauvelt is Associate
Professor of Graphic Design at North
Carolina State University, Raleigh and
is interim chair of graphic design at
Cranbrook Academy of Art, Bloomfield
Hills, Michigan. In his spare time he
maintains a graphic design practice
and writes and lectures about design
and culture." 5

Di/sci/plinary ~~Critical~~
[Disc]ursivity Critical
TheoryryMeaning? 5

TUESDAY
MARCH 11
1997
3PM
A101

Stempel Garamond Italic
(Claude Garamond, 1532)

Apple Chicago
(Charles Bigelow, 1989)

Revue
(Colin Brignall, 1969)

Berthold Imago
(Günter Gerhard Lange, 1982)

Bayer Universal Alphabet
(Herbert Bayer, 1925)

Monotype Bembo
(A. Manutius / F. Griffo, 1495)

DIN Mittelschrift
(1950s)

1.4

The skeletons are derived from existing typefaces, hence the name Compendium. The sources range from 15th century italics to Apple Macintosh system fonts. Considering the richness of type design history, the curating and editing process – deciding which letters to incorporate – obviously had to be pretty subjective.

description

Stills from the digital documentation of the CIA Compendium project, which is an encyclopedic sans serif typeface system that celebrates the richness of letter shapes in Latin type design. The 700 characters are based on sources ranging from 15th-century italics to Apple systems fonts, redrawn as monochrome sans serif letters. All share the same physical proportions, which makes them interchangeable.

dimensions

640 x 480 pixels

artwork title

CIA Compendium Interface

typefaces

CIA Antigill, CIA Dictator, CIA Dogsear, CIA Earthworm, CIA Humdrum, and CIA Oddjob

designer

Jens Gehlhaar

design company

Jens Gehlhaar

country of origin

USA

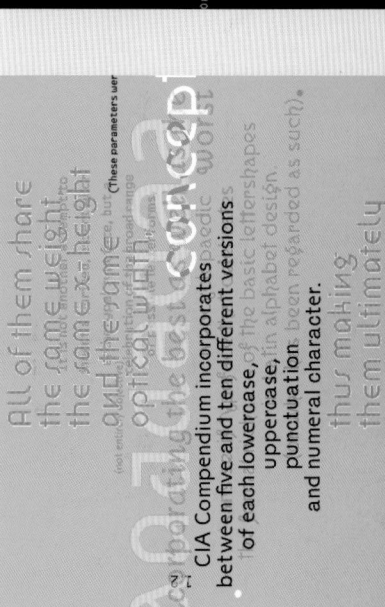

abcdefghijklmnopqrstuvwxyz

abcdefghijklmnopqrstuvwxyz

abcdefghijklmnopqrstuvwxyz

abcdefghijklmnopqrstuvwxyz

abcdefghijklmnopqrstuvwxyz

abcdefghijklmnopqrstuvwxyz

constance penley

VISITING ARTIST
CALARTS
(PROGRAM OF PHOTOGRAPHY)
LECTURE SERIES

CONSTANCE PENLEY IS A **FEMINIST WRITER** AND **THEORIST**

**LANGLEY
NOON**
12PM

**MONDAY
FEB 10**
1997

artwork title
Constance Penley

typefaces
PP Foucault and Antique Olive

designer
Jens Gehlhaar

design company
Jens Gehlhaar

illustrator
Jens Gehlhaar

country of origin
USA

description
A poster for a lecture on pornography
by Constance Penley, in the photography
program at the California Institute of
the Arts. The sexual pattern was inspired
by wallpaper from 70s soft porn movies.
With its custom-made headline typeface, the partially hidden "XXX," and
a suggestion of the male gaze, the
poster evokes the atmosphere of
adult movie theaters.

dimensions
711 x 559 mm
28 x 22 in

abcdefghijklmnopqrstuvwxyz

1234567890!@¢&*()¤?

ABCDEFGHIJKLMNOPQRSTUVWXYZ

typeface

PP Foucault

typeface family
Le Pretension Project™

designer
Jens Gehlhaar

foundry/supplier
Jens Gehlhaar

country of origin
USA

151

abcdefg

GOODY WAS DESIGNED AS AN

GOODY

Nº 124 Roman
Nº 124 SMALL CAPS
Nº 124 Cursive

Just like Fred Goudy drew some of his italics years after the roman, Goody Nº 126 Cursive was designed more than a year after the SciArc journal had been published. While the roman is loosely based on Goudy's 1921 Newstyle design, the cursive is a hybrid of the italics of Goudy Old Style, Deepdene and Truesdell.

Goody was designed by Jens Gehlhaar in 1996–97

[1]

artwork title
Goody Hype Page

typefaces
Goody No.124 Roman, Goody No.125
Small Caps, and Goody No.126
Cursive

designer
Jens Gehlhaar

design company
Jens Gehlhaar

country of origin
USA

description
The Goody typefaces were designed
as an homage to Frederic W. Goudy,
an influential 20th-century type
designer. The typefaces shown here
bring together all the quirky, clumsy,
or odd characters in Goudy's back
catalog, with some specially invented
ones. The font was originally created
in 1996 to be used in a publication
for the Southern California Institute
of Architecture.

dimensions
216 x 279 mm
8¹/₂ x 11 in

hijklmn   stuvwxyz

ABCDEFGHIJKLMNOPQRSTUVWXYZ

1234567890!@&*()"?

typeface

**Goody No. 124
Roman**

typeface family
Goody

designer
Jens Gehlhaar

foundry/supplier
Jens Gehlhaar

country of origin
USA

opqr

typeface
Laika Book Roman

typeface family
Laika

designer
Jens Gehlhaar

foundry/supplier
Jens Gehlhaar

country of origin
USA

Bachelor of Fine Arts

The Bachelor of Fine Arts degree in Dance is awarded to those young emerging artists who have shown full understanding of the principles of dance technique, acquired experience in concert production, and created a body of choreographic work in at least one group-form and one solo-form composition, which must be produced in one of the Dance School's many diverse presentations. Students must give evidence of a competent performing presence, within their own limits, and of the self-discipline and self-motivation needed to succeed in a professional career in dance art.

The BFA degree is conferred when a student successfully completes the dance program of study and performance, completes all Critical Studies requirements, and meets the Institute minimum of 120 completed semester units. All judgments concerning eligibility for any degree or certificate are made by the dance faculty as a whole. Every BFA student is required to take two technique classes (one in ballet and one in modern dance) four days each week. Each undergraduate is required to enroll in one of four levels of composition class offered each semester. Each student must reach the highest level of his/her ability in modern or ballet technique (i.e. level 3) by the fourth year and an upper division composition level (at least level 3) before being considered for graduation, as well as completing all crew assignments. In addition, fourth-year students work on independent projects with their mentor, who is responsible for guiding these projects. All choreographic work that is to be performed under the auspices of the School of Dance must be shown to the faculty and student body for critique and guidance prior to performance. Dance Showings are held weekly and must be attended by every dance student. Work is shown at every stage—from short, simple phrases to more complex, finished compositions. Vital to the presentation of dance performance are all of those skills offered in the School of Theatre's program in Performing Arts Design, Technology, and Management. Therefore, each undergraduate student is required to enroll in a year-long course in the fundamental skills of theatrical presentation, such as basic principles of lighting design, sound design, video, costuming, makeup, and management. In order to fully utilize these basic principles, students are also required to take advanced courses in the development of concepts of lighting, costume design, and the creation of physical environments. Apart from the course requirements in design and technology, every student is assigned at least two crew positions during each year of residence at CalArts.

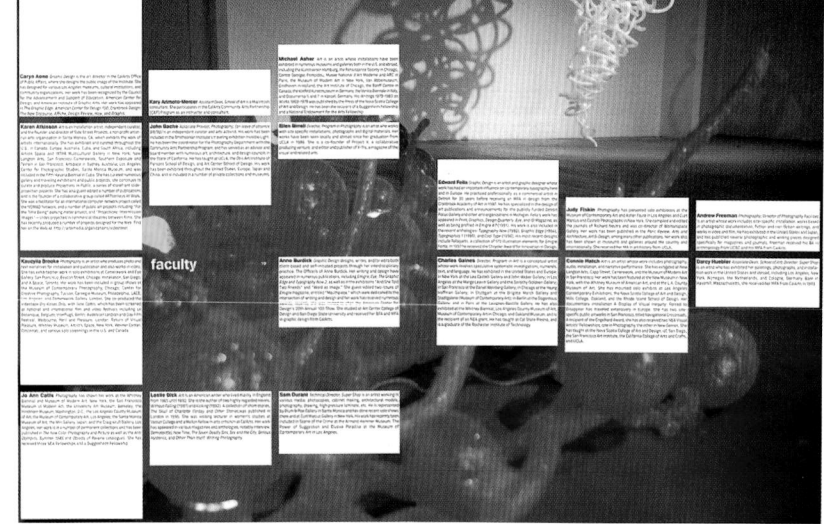

abcdefghijklmnopqrstuvwxyz

1234567890!@&*()"?ABCDEFGHIJKLMNOPQRSTUVWXYZ

5
Melissa Spooner, on right, in Spring Music Festival

6
Spring Dance Concert

7
Linda Park performing in Sacja Chaiyasate's dance thesis concert

Master of Fine Arts

The Master of Fine Arts program in the School of Dance has an emphasis in choreography and is intended for those talented applicants who demonstrate an aptitude for dance making and who have a desire to continue to work as choreographers in the professional field. The Master of Fine Arts degree is conferred when a student completes, with distinction, a thesis concert and all other requirements at the graduate level of his or her second year. The curriculum is designed to help students in the development of their own personal aesthetic. Course work is taught on a seminar basis with focus on organization of concepts, artistic and career goals as well as emphasis on the practical realization of mounting a concert. In the first year of the Master's Program all MFA students present a combined evening of their work. The emphasis of this concert is on solo work, although it is not limited to only solo work. Many students present work which is solo-based but has other components of group work. However, it is expected that each graduate student choreograph in solo form. The support, critique and procedural preparation of this concert is the same as for the thesis concert except it is a shared experience for all first-year graduate students. The thesis concert is produced in the second year of residence (or third for those students who feel they need the extra time and obtain faculty approval). Graduate students have a choice of producing their work in the first or second semester of the second year. This arrangement insures that there will be sufficient numbers of dancers available as both cast and crew and that there will be adequate time for rehearsal and critique. Each graduate student is required to have an open audition which the entire Dance School student body is eligible to attend.

Every graduate student must also submit a written thesis outline to the faculty for approval. This outline must be accepted by the faculty before major work is begun on the thesis. Graduate students are required to sign a contract stating they will honor all guidelines in the production of their concert and must stay within the required budget.

MFA students must present their work in Dance Showings in order to have it viewed periodically by both students and faculty. At these times, the graduate student is expected to be able to discuss his/her choreographic concepts in a clear, concise manner so that ideas and information can be freely exchanged.

The Dance School expects graduate students to be role models for undergraduates, setting examples in leadership and discipline, as well as in creative work. Graduate assistantships reflect the need for very responsible students. The graduate program is at the very core of the Dance School. The work of the graduate student helps to advance the abilities of the undergraduates. It is essential to our objectives that we maintain a very high caliber of graduate students who are capable of both leading and learning from the entire dance community.

Candidates for the MFA degree take daily technique classes with undergraduate candidates and enroll in composition courses during each year of residency. First-year MFA students are required to take **Modern Technique**, **Composition III**, **Production Seminar**, **Concepts in Lighting Design for Dance**, **Video for Dance**, **Digital Dance**, **MFA-I Project**, **Music & the 20th Century**, **Clothing and Form**, **Thesis Workshop** and **Graduate Production Crewing**. The second-year MFA course requirements, in addition to **Modern Technique**, are **Composition IV**, **Thesis Workshop**, **MFA-II Thesis Project**, **Music & the 20th Century**, **Production Seminar**, **Digital Dance**, and **Graduate Production Crewing**. **Ballet** is an elective for graduate students during their tenure in the Dance Program.

The graduate student's participation in the Dance Program gives each student hands-on experience in the organization, teaching, and artistic creation of dance. We have four graduate assistantships that carry a one-half tuition stipend. Two are as production managers for the Dance School's theatre (Theatre II) and two are as costume coordinators. In order to apply for these positions (after one has been accepted into the program), the graduate student must have had prior documented experience in either area of expertise. There are six additional assistantship positions. They are: two for Institute dance, one for publicity, one for video, one for sound, and one for editor of the Dance School Newsletter.

artwork title
California Institute of the Arts
Catalog 1999–2002

typefaces
Laika, PP Lacan, AG Book Stencil,
and Microsoft Georgia

designers
Geoff McFetridge and
Michael Worthington

design companies
Champion Graphics and
Worthington Design

photographers
Steven A. Gunther, Scott Groller,
Rachel Slowinski, and Evan
Merryman Ritter

country of origin
USA

description
This prospectus attempts to portray
the California Institute of the Arts
as an energetic, exciting place to
go to school, while at the same
time stressing the hard work and
dedication needed to succeed. The
underlying theme was "organic
technology" and how it applies to
the various arts disciplines at CalArts.

dimensions
216 x 273 mm
8¹/₂ x 10³/₄ in

12345

ABCDEFGHIJKLMNOPQRSTUVWXYZ

typeface
**Pace Impact
Heavy**

typeface family
Pace Impact

designer
Michael Chang Winterberg

foundry/supplier
Pacesetters

country of origin
Denmark

abcdefghijklmnopqrstuvwxyz

!□?

artwork title
Cleese Festival Program

typefaces
Pace Impact and Pace 242

designers
Michael Chang Winterberg
and Claus Collstrup

design company
Pacesetters

country of origin
Denmark

description
The cover for a festival program,
which was inspired by the idea of
letting Terry Gilliam loose on a
computer. A xerox machine proved
invaluable in the creation process.

dimensions
180 x 180 mm
7^1/$_4$ x 7^1/$_4$ in

JOHN CLEESE SOCIETY OF ÅRHUS OG OMEGN
PRÆSENTERER VERDENS STØRSTE

C LEE S E
FE ST IV AL

ÅRHUS FESTUGE 1998 FRA 28. AUGUST TIL 6. SEPTEMBER

7890

artwork title
Cleese Festival Program

typefaces
Pace Impact and Pace 242

designers
Michael Chang Winterberg
and Claus Collstrup

design company
Pacesetters

country of origin
Denmark

description
Two interior pages of the festival
program, as on previous spread.

dimensions
360 x 180 mm
14^1/$_2$ x 7^1/$_4$ in

ET TOSSET PROGRAM

Vi mener, at denne festuges tema, Danske visioner, er som skabt til en hel uges John Cleese-happening. Det er ingen tilfældighed, at Cleeses nok mest trofaste publikum findes i Danmark. Således kan fremhæves Stand up homage to Cleese, hvor danske komikere hver aften kl. 23.00 betaler af på udlandsgælden i et timelangt show - med blandt andet teatersport over det 13. afsnit af Halløj på badehotellet, der skrives af gæsterne på Åbent Åndværksteds pc´ere i løbet af ugen. Desuden kan man spille pythonsk minigolf, surfe på en guidet Cleese-tur på Internet, spille Python CD-rom spil, ligesom vort museum, Hall of relics , kan fremvise den ske, som efter al sandsynlighed er identisk med den, som Manuel blev gokket med.

Hertil kommer mange andre uheldige indslag:

Serveringsteater - Sorry we are out of Walldorfs, duck and trifle
Fællesaften med Dansk Monty Python Forening fra København.
Peep-show
Åbent Åndværksted
Zoo - med bl.a. Siberean Hamster
Optog i gakkede gangarter
Miss Tibbs Tea Room m. kage og ønskebiograf
Fotostat, hvor man kan blive fotograferet med Cleese

abcdefghijklmnopqrstuvwxyz
1234567890!@&*()?
ABCDEFGHIJKLMNOPQRSTUVWXYZ

ET REFUGIUM I FESTUGEN

Festivalen og Cleese-cafeen henvender sig til alle, der trænger til et sted at slappe lidt af i den ofte planløse vandring mellem gade-aktiviteter og udskænkningssteder, såvel som de, der nøje planlægger deres deltagelse i festugen gennem det officielle festugeprogram. Der bliver kun et par programsatte underholdningsarrangementer om dagen, så man kan ikke komme for sent; det skal være uforpligtende at lægge vejen forbi en Cleese-festival. Gæsterne skal i vid udstrækning selv opsøge morskaben, og overraskelsen er vigtig. Vi vil således pythonisere omgivelserne fra indgangen i gården til tårnværelset oppe over penthouse'et.

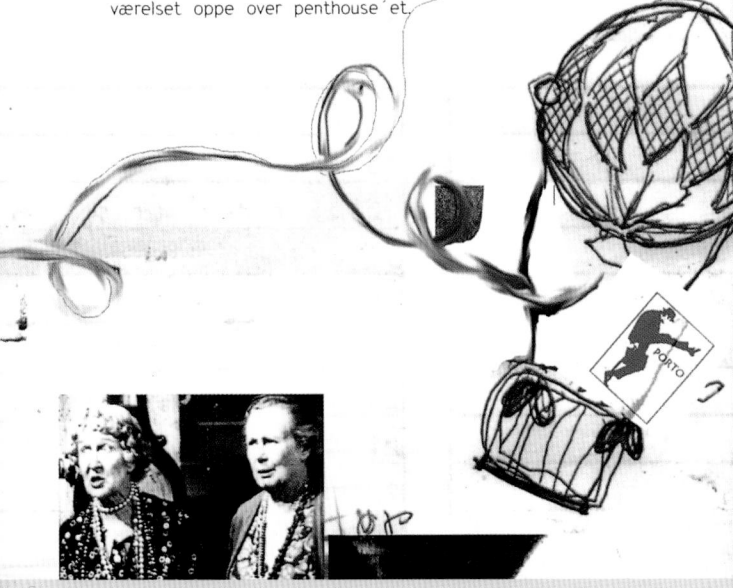

typeface
Pace 242
Regular
typeface family
Pace 242

designer
Claus Collstrup

foundry/supplier
Pacesetters

country of origin
Denmark

typeface
Scissor

typeface family
Scissor

designer
Eric Zimm

foundry/supplier
Small Icon

country of origin
USA

abcdefghi
jklmnopqr
stuvwxyz

ABCDEFGHIJKLMNOPQRSTUVWXYZ

1234567890!@&*()"?

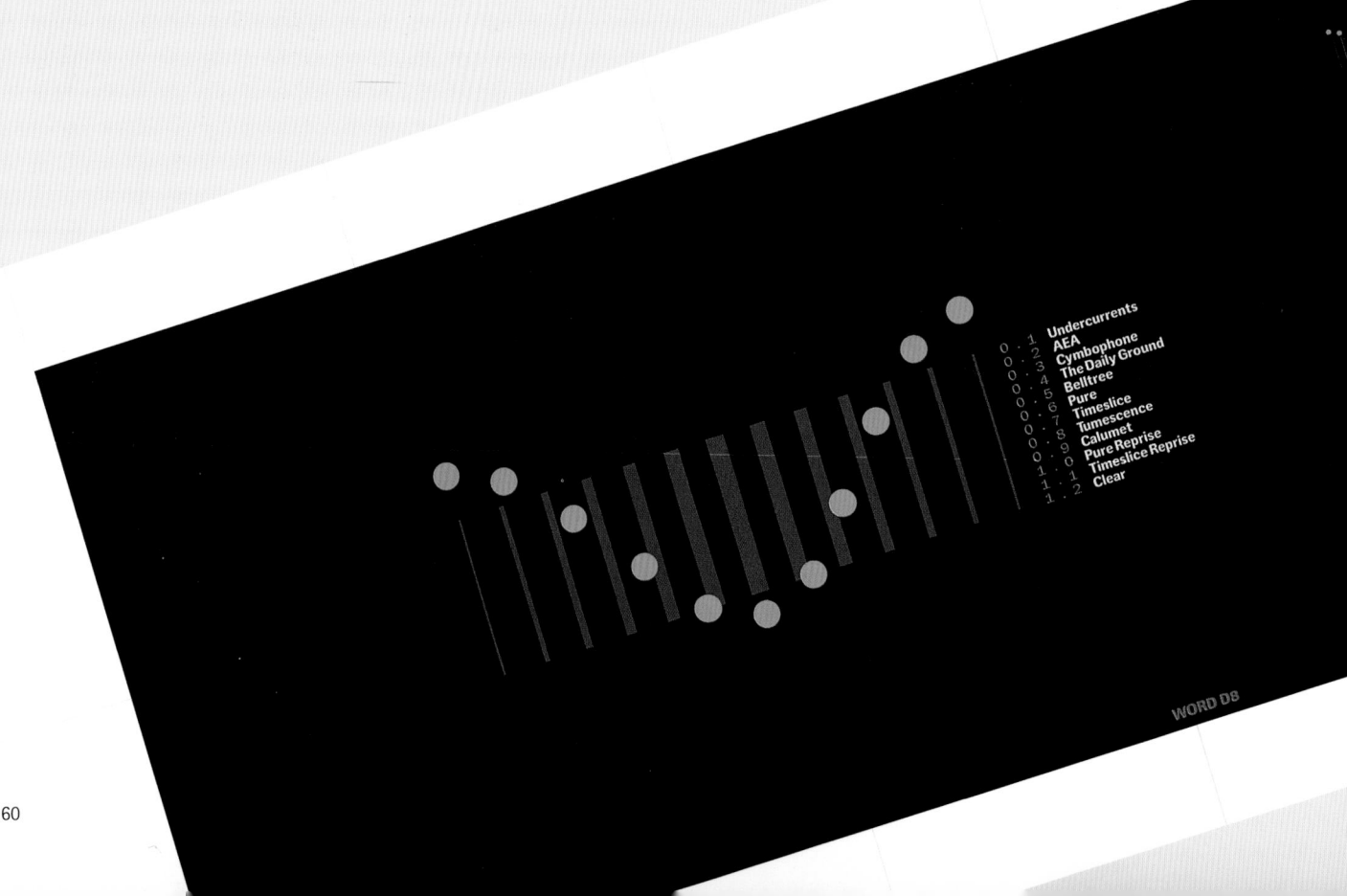

artwork title
Internal Clock

typeface
Scissor

designer
Michael Faulkner

design company
RawPaw Graphics

country of origin
UK

description
CD concertina for Circadian Rhythms, depicting the northern solstice. The concept behind the "Internal Clock" CD was time, and it took a long time for the project to come to fruition: three years for the music and six months for the design.

dimensions
Concertina:
360 x 120 mm, 14^1/$_8$ x 4^3/$_4$ in
CD: 120 mm, 4^3/$_4$ in diameter

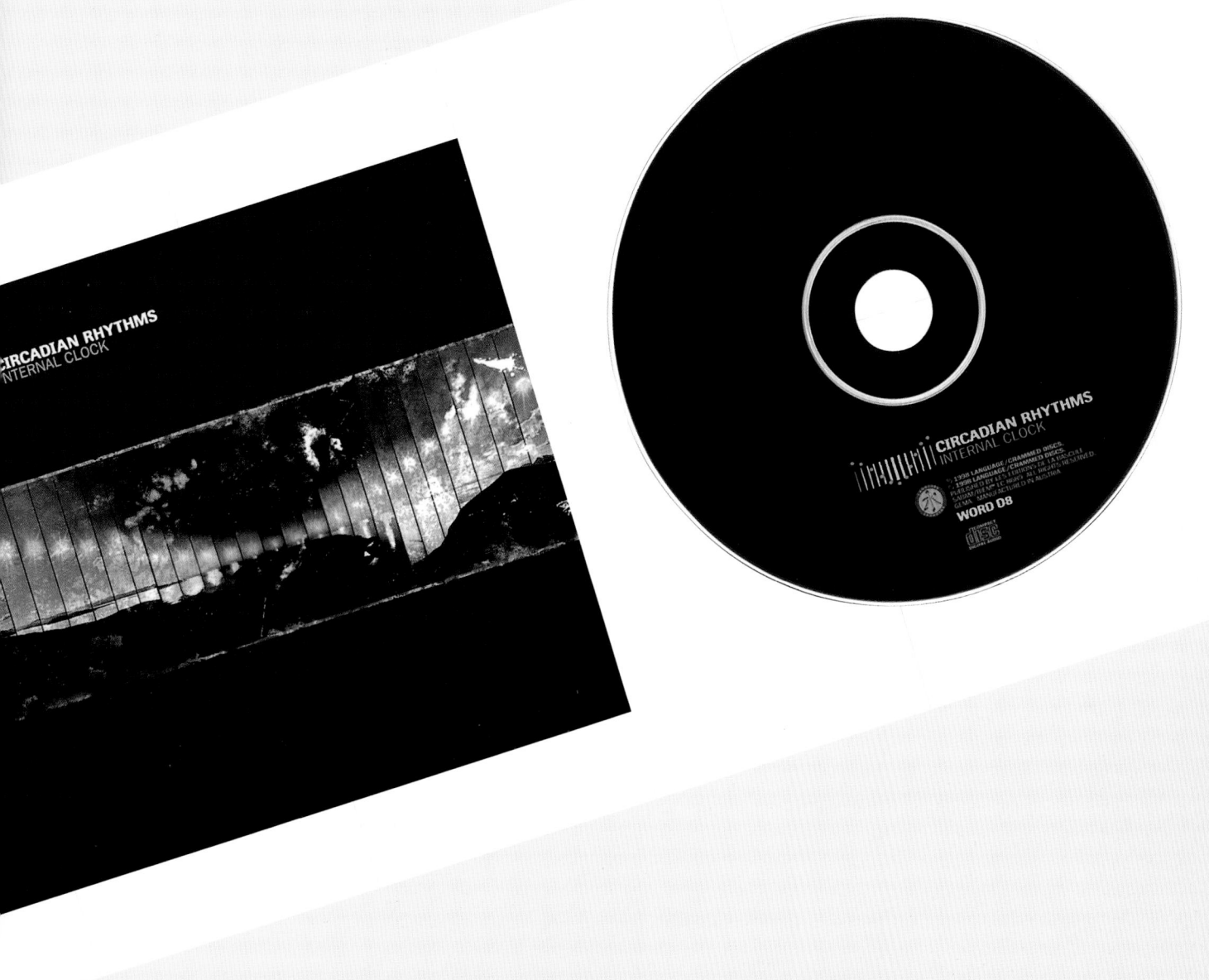

SilentMail Nineteen-Ninety-Eight

Jens Gehlhaar	Pirco Wolfframm	Tracy Hopcus	Snow Kahn	Dennis Toyoda	Ana Llorente Thurk	Chris Selby	Huee Min Loi	Jani Soderlund	Adam King	(Dave Enomoto)
MOP	DN	KJL	RTZ	AQ	BE IS	GW	Uy	FV	CHX	
ans	dir	ex	ku	hw	pf	clz	jqt	pv	by	gmo

45pt
The quick brown fox jumps over the lazy dog (.,;' "")

45pt
THE QUICK BROWN FOX JUMPS OVER THE LAZY DOG.

18/19.5pt
Situated in the external zone of the Milky Way, the Sun takes about two hundred million years to make a complete revolution of the Galaxy. Right, that's how long it takes, not a day less, Qrwrfq said, once, as I went past, I drew a sign at a point in space, just so I could find it again two hundred million years later, when we went

14/16.5pt
Situated in the external zone of the Milky Way, the Sun takes about two hundred million years to make a complete revolution of the Galaxy. Right, that's how long it takes, not a day less, Qrwrfq said, once, as I went past, I drew a sign at a point in space, just so I could find it again two hundred million years later, when we went by the next time around. What sort of sign. It's hard to explain because if I say sign to you, you immediately think of a something that can be distinguished from a

10/13.5pt
Situated in the external zone of the Milky Way, the Sun takes about two hundred million years to make a complete revolution of the Galaxy. Right, that's how long it takes, not a day less, Qrwrfq said, once, as I went past, I drew a sign at a point in space, just so I could find it again two hundred million years later, when we went by the next time around. What sort of sign. It's hard to explain because if I say sign to you, you immediately think of a something that can be distinguished from a something else, but nothing could be distinguished from anything there; you immediately think of a sign made with some implement or with your hands, and then when you take the implement or your hands away, the sign remains, but in those days there were no implements or even hands, or teeth, or noses, all things that came along afterwards, a long time afterwards. As to the

7.5/10pt
Situated in the external zone of the Milky Way, the Sun takes about two hundred million years to make a complete revolution of the Galaxy. Right, that's how long it takes, not a day less, Qrwrfq said, once, as I went past, I drew a sign at a point in space, just so I could find it again two hundred million years later, when we went by the next time around. What sort of sign. It's hard to explain because if I say sign to you, you immediately think of a something that can be distinguished from a something else, but nothing could be distinguished from anything there; you immediately think of a sign made with some implement or with your hands, and then when you take the implement or your hands away, the sign remains, but in those days there were no implements or even hands, or teeth, or noses, all things that came along afterwards, a long time afterwards. As to the form a sign should have, you say it's no problem because, whatever

8/12pt
SITUATED IN THE EXTERNAL ZONE OF THE MILKY WAY, THE SUN TAKES ABOUT TWO HUNDRED MILLION YEARS TO MAKE A COMPLETE REVOLUTION OF THE GALAXY. RIGHT, THAT'S HOW LONG IT TAKES, NOT A DAY LESS, QRWRFQ SAID, ONCE, AS I WENT PAST, I DREW A SIGN AT A POINT IN SPACE, JUST

artwork title
Silent Mail Specimen

typeface
Silent Mail Nineteen-Ninety-Eight

designer
Jens Gehlhaar

college
California Institute of the Arts

country of origin
USA

description
Sample from a "letter lottery," where each student draws lots to design five to six characters for a typeface. One student receives six letters from the instructor; then, based on the formal parameters defined by these six letters, the student creates the characters assigned to them in the letter lottery. Finally, they erase the first six letters and hand the newly designed ones to the next student, who repeats the process until each student has designed their allotted characters and the typeface is complete.

dimensions
430 x 280 mm
17 x 11 in

typeface

Silent Mail Nineteen- Ninety-Eight

typeface family
Silent Mail Nineteen-Ninety-Eight

designers
David Enomoto, Tracy Hopcus, Snow Kahn, Adam King, Ana Llorente-Thurik, Hwee Min Loi, Chris Selby, Jani Soderlund, Dennis Toyoda, Pirco Wolfframm, and Jens Gehlhaar

foundry/supplier
not available for commercial use

country of origin
USA

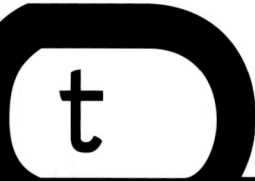

abcdefghijklmnopqrstuvwxyz
ABCDEFGHIJKLMNOPQRSTUVWXYZ

Relativeren:
Irma Boom and
Max Bruinsma
in conversation

Tickets available from Freda Sack
Studio 12
10–11 Archer Street
London W1V 7HG
T 0171 734 6925

Cheques payable to
Society of Typographic Designers
Enclose a dl sae
std members £8.00
non-members £10.00

6.30 pm
Thursday December 4th 1997
RIBA
66 Portland Place
London W1N 4AD

std lecture series 97

This last lecture in the **std** year on Dutch design will include an overview of the series which has featured:
Julius Vermeulen, Commissioner of Design for ptt; Wim Crouwel and Jan van Toorn, designers and educators;
and Hans Bockting and Will de l'Ecluse partners in UNA design group.
Please bring any relevant questions on Dutch design issues for discussion at the Irma Boom lecture.
The Dutch lectures will form the basis of the 98 spring/summer issue of Typographic, the std Journal,
designed by UNA in Amsterdam with an introduction by Max Bruinsma.
Non-members can order copies in advance.

artwork title
Relativeren

typeface
Foundry Form Sans

designer
David Quay

design company
The Foundry

country of origin
UK

description
An invitation for a lecture on
Dutch design, organized by the
Society of Typographic Designers.

dimensions
210 x 150 mm
8^1/$_4$ x 5^7/$_8$ in

ABCDEF

GHIJKLM

NOPQRST

UVWXYZ

1234567890

abcdef

ghijklm

nopqrst

uvwxyz

typeface
**Foundry Form
Sans Book**

typeface family
Foundry Form Sans

designer
David Quay

foundry/supplier
The Foundry

country of origin
UK

ABCDEFG
HIJKLM
NOPQRST
UVWXYZ

1234567890!@&*( )"?

abcdefghijklmnopqrstuvwxyz

typeface

Foundry Gridnik Regular

typeface family
Foundry Gridnik

designers
Wim Crouwel/The Foundry

foundry/supplier
The Foundry

country of origin
UK

Foundry Gridnik Light
Foundry Gridnik Regular
Foundry Gridnik Medium
Foundry Gridnik Bold

Foundry Gridnik

Foundry Gridnik is available
for both Mac and PC and can
be purchased directly from
The Foundry designers↦

For more information about
Foundry Gridnik or other
Foundry typefaces, contact
the designers, David Quay or
Freda Sack at the address
opposite↦

The Foundry
Studio 12
10–11 Archer Street
London W1V 7HG
England

t 44 (0)171 734 6925
f 44 (0)171 734 2607
e dqfs@thefoundrystudio.co.uk

Foundry Gridnik, described as 'the thinking man's Courier', derives from a typeface
that was originally designed by Dutch designer Wim Crouwel in the late 60s, as a single
weight typewriter face, but it was never released as a font↦

A modified version of it can still be seen today on Crouwel's 1976 designs for the
low-value postage stamps of the ppt, Dutch post office, which feature the stamp
value only, displaying the numerals to full effect↦

The Foundry has named the typeface Gridnik because of Crouwel's devotion to
grids and systems in his work to create visual order; he was often affectionately
referred to in the 60s as 'Mr Gridnik' by his friends and contemporaries↦

**Foundry Gridnik was originally released in a single weight font as one of six
typefaces in Foundry Architype 3, Crouwel Collection, Foundry Gridnik has now
been extended by The Foundry designers into a family of four weights, with
the full approval of Crouwel↦**

artwork title
Foundry Gridnik

typeface
Foundry Gridnik

designer
David Quay

design company
The Foundry

country of origin
UK

description
Promotional flyer for the
Foundry Gridnik typeface

dimensions
210 x 100 mm
$8^1/_4$ x $3^7/_8$ in

BIOTYPOGRAPHY

TOBY STOKES

S CARABEUS SACER is remarkable for the parental care that it bestows on its offspring. The same characteristic is found not only in other members of the genus but in certain species of related genera as well.

The scarabs actions are entirely instinctive but it is not at all surprising that in ancient times man believed not only that the scarab was capable of rational behaviour but was governed by supernatural forces. It follows naturally that it became an object of worship.

artwork title
Biotypography

typefaces
Beetle and Formica

designer
Toby Stokes

design company
Medium Rare Ltd.

photographer
Toby Stokes

illustrator
Toby Stokes

country of origin
UK

description
The cover and an interior spread from *Biotypography*, a 48-page paperback, which explores the effects of evolution on letterforms by applying biogenetic theories to type design and classification.

dimensions
Cover:
181 x 111 mm, 7 1/8 x 4 3/8 in
Spread:
362 x 111 mm, 14 1/4 x 4 3/8 in

typeface

Beetle

typeface family
Beetle

designer
Toby Stokes

foundry/supplier
Medium Rare Ltd.

country of origin
UK

abcdefghijklmnopqrstuvwxyz
1234567890!@&*()"?

ABCDEFGHIJKLMNOPQRSTUVWXYZ

abcdef
ghijklmno
pqrstuv
wxyz

1234567890!@&*()"?

ABCDEFGHIJK
LMNOPQRSTUVWXYZ

typeface

Formica

typeface family
Formica

designer
Toby Stokes

foundry/supplier
Medium Rare Ltd.

country of origin
UK

The ants took naturally to their new habitat on the page, quickly delegating workers to separate paragraphs, with scouts making occasional brief forays into the margins. I sat back and observed what the ants would make of their new unfamiliar employees. As fortune would have it, the ants began to work *with a renewed urgency.*

I expect it may still take a while longer before this colony is firmly settled and established. But so began the parasitic, or perhaps symbiotic relationship that I have appreciated ever since to be a feature under domestication of these creatures.

"*Go to the ant,* thou sluggard, *consider her ways,* and be wise." Proverbs [6.6] Solomon

artwork title
Biotypography

typefaces
Beetle and Formica

designer
Toby Stokes

design company
Medium Rare Ltd.

photographer
Toby Stokes

illustrator
Toby Stokes

country of origin
UK

description
Interior, as on previous spread

dimensions
Spread:
362 x 111 mm, 14^{1}/$_{4}$ x 4^{3}/$_{8}$ in

abcdefghijklmnopqrstuvwxyz

ABCDEFGHIJKL

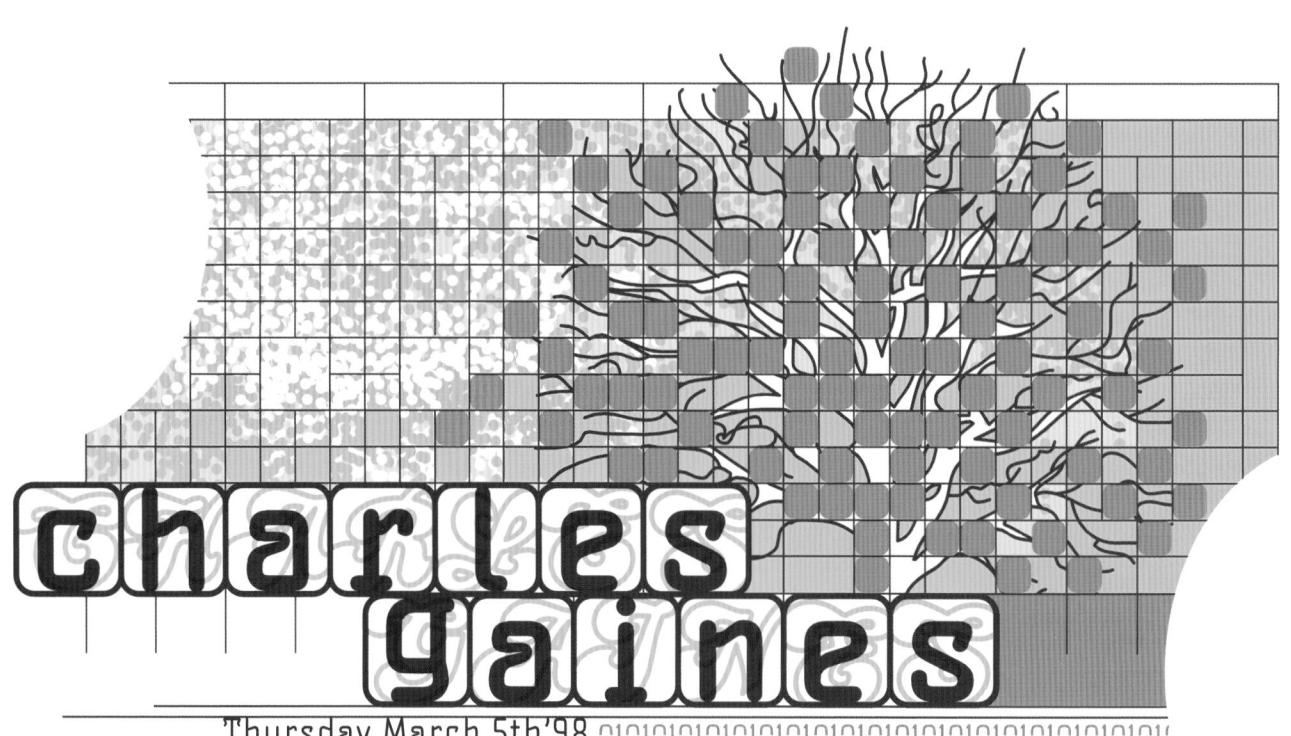

charles
gaines

Thursday March 5th'98 ololololololololololololololololololololololololol
ololololololololololololol CalArts ololololololololololololololololol
ololololololololololololololololololol Art Department Faculty
Lecture Series ololololololol 7pm olololololololololololololol F 200 ololololololol

MΠΩ0PQRSTUVШXYZ

Left:

Left:

artwork title
Charles Gaines

typefaces
Morris Bold, Morris Regular,
Candice, and Luna

designer
Andrea Tinnes

college
California Institute of the Arts

illustrator
Andrea Tinnes

country of origin
USA

description
A poster for a lecture by Charles
Gaines at the California Institute
of the Arts.

dimensions
610 x 840 mm
24 x 33 in

Above:

artwork title
Family Affair

typefaces
Morris Regular, Arnold Böcklin,
Bureau Agency, Otto, Isonorm,
Jackson, and Jacky

designer
Andrea Tinnes

college
California Institute of the Arts

photographers
Andrea Tinnes and family members

illustrator
Andrea Tinnes

country of origin
USA/Germany

description
A double spread from the thesis
"Family Affair—a family album of
font marriages." A project at the
California Institute of the Arts, this
work explores the genetics of
typefaces by applying the basic
principles of biogenetics, such as
the breeding and crossing of
dominant and recessive character
traits, to font design.

dimensions
255 x 195 mm
10 x 7⁵/₈ in

typeface
Morris Regular

typeface family
Morris

designer
Andrea Tinnes

foundry/supplier
Andrea Tinnes

country of origin
USA/Germany

1234567890

typeface

Rudolf Jr Bold

typeface family
Rudolf Jr

designer
Andrea Tinnes

foundry/supplier
Andrea Tinnes

country of origin
USA/Germany

artwork title
Family Affair

typefaces
Rudolf Jr, Edda, Colin, Alessandro,
Susan, Lunatix, Kabel, Revue,
Quirinus, Memphis, Nova Script,
Outwest, and Parisian

designer
Andrea Tinnes

college
California Institute of the Arts

photographers
Karl Tinnes and José Allard

illustrator
Andrea Tinnes

country of origin
USA

description
as on previous spread

dimensions
255 x 195 mm
10 x 7⅝ in

abcdefghijklmnopqrstuvwxyz
ABCDEFGHIJKLMNOPQRSTUVWXYZ
1234567890

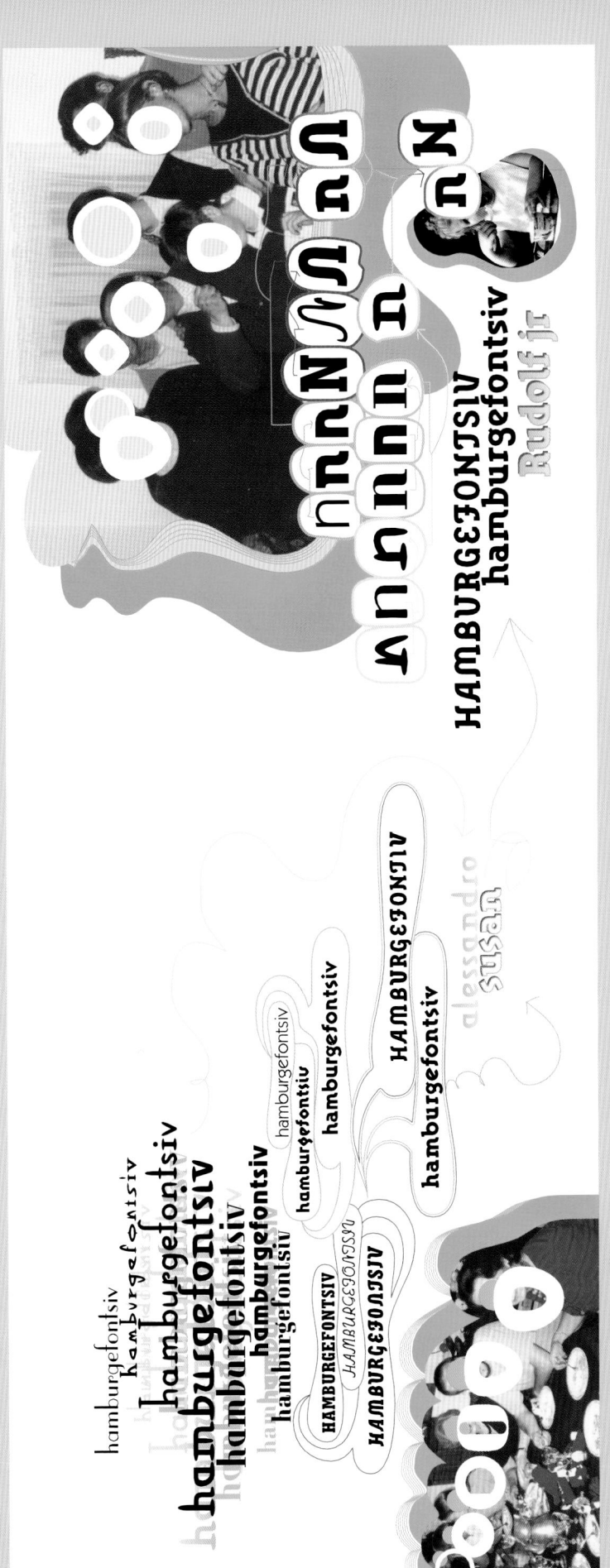

AaBbCcDd€eFf

1234561890€¢$

@™ß&?!ﮒﺔﺓﺓ

AaBbCcDd€eFf

1234561890€¢$

@™ß&?!ﮒﺔﺓﺓ

AaBbCcDd€eFf

1234561890€¢$

@™ß&?!ﮒﺔﺓﺓ

CousCous to the People

Falafel to the People

Kabob to the People

abc

ograbic

Get it online @

www.fountain.nu

1234567890!@&*[]"?

abcdefg

hijklmnopqrs

tuvwxyz

ABCDEFGHIJK

MNOPQRSTUVWXYZ

artwork title
Promotional image

typeface
OGRAbic

designer
Simon Schmidt

design company
Simon Schmidt

country of origin
Germany

description
A promotional image for OGRAbic,
a typeface designed for use in
printed publications and websites.

dimensions
105 x 170 mm
4^1/$_8$ x 6^3/$_4$ in

typeface

OGRAbic Kebab

typeface family
OGRA

designer
Simon Schmidt

foundry/supplier
Fountain

country of origin
Germany

ABCDEF

ABCDEFGHIJKLMNOPQRSI

GHIJKL

MNOPQR

STUVWX

YZ1

234

typeface

OGRA Regular

typeface family
OGRA

designer
Simon Schmidt

foundry/supplier
Fountain

country of origin
Germany

UVWXYZ

artwork title
Gott

typeface
OGRA

designer
Simon Schmidt

design company
Simon Schmidt

photographer
Simon Schmidt

country of origin
Germany

description
A book cover design for a
novel by Thorsten Ehrenberg.

dimensions
105 x 160 mm
4¹/₈ x 6¹/₄ in

0123456789

artwork title
Beatlab Cover

typeface
OGRA

art director
Stefan Rekittke

designer
Simon Schmidt

design company
Simon Schmidt

country of origin
Germany

description
A CD cover for a compilation
by Superstition Records.

dimensions
121 x 120 mm
4³/₄ x 4³/₄ in

Visual Index of Typefaces

All index entries refer to pages on which captions appear.

* indicates a typeface, which at the time of going to press, was not yet digitized.

Index of Typefaces

Index of Designers

Index of Foundries/ Suppliers

ACME fonts
4 Regent House, 109–111 Britannia
Walk, London N1 7ND, UK
Tel and Fax: +44 171 490 7877

Atsushi Aoki
837-2 Wado Miyasiro-Machi
Minamisaitama-gun Saitama
345-0836, Japan
Tel: +81 480 32 3823

Apply Design Group
Krugstrasse 16, D-30453 Hannover,
Germany
Tel: +49 511 485 02 98
Fax: +49 511 485 02 99

Attention Earthling
1299 Palmer Avenue #210, Larchmont,
NY 10538, USA
Tel: +1 914 834 9429

brass_fonts cologne
Friesenwall 24, D-50672 Köln, Germany
Tel: +49 221 257 77 55
Fax: +49 221 257 77 03

bulldozer®editions
88 bis rue Faubourg du Temple,
75011 Paris, France
Tel: +33 1 53 36 77 34/35
Fax: +33 1 53 36 77 31
e-mail: bulldozer@bleu-elastique.com

büro destruct
Wasserwerkgasse 7, CH-3011,
Bern, Switzerland
Tel: +41 31 312 63 83
Fax: +41 31 312 63 07

Editable Graphics
Tel: +1 303 466 4342
Fax: +1 303 466 3180
http://www.editablegraphics.com

Face2Face
Nollendorfstrasse 11/12, D-10777
Berlin, Germany
Tel: +49 30 215 00 88
Fax: +49 30 215 00 89

Sean Fermoyle c/o simpletype
1250 North Lasalle #1108, Chicago,
IL 60610, USA

fontBoy
183 the Alameda, San Anselmo,
CA 94960, USA
Tel: +1 415 721 7921
Fax: +1 415 721 7965
http://www.fontboy.com

FontShop International
Bergmannstrasse 102, D-10691 Berlin,
Germany
Tel: +49 30 693 70 22
Fax: +49 30 692 84 43

FontWorks UK Ltd.
65-69 East Road, London N1 6AH, UK
Tel: +44 171 490 2002
Fax: +44 171 608 1224

The Foundry
Studio 12, 10-11 Archer Street,
London W1V 7HG, UK
Tel: +44 171 734 6925
Fax: +44 171 734 2607

Fountain
Södraparkgatan 29A, SE-214 22
Malmö, Sweden
http://www.fountain.nu
e-mail: info@fountain.nu

Jens Gehlhaar
436 North Ogden Drive #2,
Los Angeles, CA 90036, USA
Tel: +1 323 655 6230
Fax: +1 323 655 6235
e-mail: jensg@earthlink.net

International Typeface Corporation
228 East 45th Street, 12th Floor,
New York, NY 10017, USA
Tel: +1 212 949 8072

j-buyers.com
Tel and Fax: +44 171 608 0854
e-mail: bigson@j-buyers.com

The Letterbox
Suite One, 7th Floor, 289 Flinders Lane,
Melbourne 3000, Australia
Tel: +61 3 9650 6433
Fax: +61 3 9650 5211

Hwee Min Loi
4320 South Centinela Ave #105,
Los Angeles, CA 90066, USA
Tel: +1 310 313 2823
e-mail: hweeminloi@hotmail.com

Medium Rare Ltd.
41 Clink Street Studios, Clink Street,
London SE1 9DG, UK
Tel: +44 171 403 3395
Fax: +44 171 378 7154

NOISE
54a Elsworthy Road, London
NW3 3BU, UK
Tel: 0171 586 1171/0946

Pacesetters
Hjortensgade 1, DK-8000 Aarhus C,
Denmark
Tel: +45 87 30 33 37
Fax: +45 87 30 33 38

popglory
e-mail: popglory@earthlink.net

Prototype Experimental Foundry
2318 North High Street #9, Columbus,
OH 43202, USA
Tel: +1 614 447 8103
Fax: +1 614 447 8104

Psy/Ops Type Foundry
923 Folsom Street, Tank 5,
San Francisco, CA 94107, USA
Tel: +1 415 896 5788
888 PSY-FONE (only within USA)
Fax: +1 415 896 2290

RawPaw Graphics
2nd Floor, 13-14 Great Sutton Street,
London EC1V 0BX, UK
Tel: +44 171 253 3462

Lee Schulz
96 Washington Street Apartment #8,
Brighton, MA 02216, USA
e-mail: inspekt@aol.com

Chris Selby
2010 Seca Street, Elcajon,
CA 92019, USA
Tel: +1 619 447 8839

Small Icon
343 West 22nd Street #7, New York,
NY 10011, USA
Tel: +1 212 989 5147

Jeremy Tankard | Typography
c/o FontWorks UK Ltd.
65-69 East Road, London N1 6AH, UK
Tel: +44 171 490 2002
Fax: +44 171 608 1224

Andrea Tinnes
639 North Manhattan Place,
Los Angeles, CA 90004, USA
Tel: +1 323 469 0456

Virus c/o FontWorks UK Ltd.
65-69 East Road, London N1 6AH, UK
Tel: +44 171 490 2002
Fax: +44 171 608 1224

Garry Waller
70 Roding Road, London E5 0DW, UK

Pirco Wolfframm
309 Avenue C #2F, New York,
NY 10009, USA
Tel: +1 212 260 6933
e-mail: pircowolfframm@hotmail.com

YAM
56b Market Place,
London NW11 6JP, UK
Tel: +44 181 201 9955
Fax: +44 181 455 1805

Future projects

If you would like to be included in the call for entries for future projects, please send your name and address to:

Design Projects
Duncan Baird Publishers
Sixth Floor
Castle House
75–76 Wells Street
London W1P 3RE
UK

e-mail: tara@dbairdpub.co.uk